Building Smart LEGO MINDSTORMS EV3 Robots

Leverage the LEGO MINDSTORMS EV3 platform to build and program intelligent robots

Kyle Markland

Building Smart LEGO MINDSTORMS EV3 Robots

Commissioning Editor: Vijin Boricha
Acquisition Editor: Rahul Nair
Content Development Editor: Sharon Raj
Technical Editor: Komal Karne
Copy Editor: Safis Editing
Project Coordinator: Virginia Dias
Proofreader: Safis Editing
Indexer: Aishwarya Gangawane
Graphics: Tom Scaria
Production Coordinator: Aparna Bhagat

First published: April 2018

Production reference: 1020418

Published by Packt Publishing Ltd.
Livery Place
35 Livery Street
Birmingham
B3 2PB, UK.

ISBN 978-1-78847-156-5

www.packtpub.com

`mapt.io`

Mapt is an online digital library that gives you full access to over 5,000 books and videos, as well as industry leading tools to help you plan your personal development and advance your career. For more information, please visit our website.

Why subscribe?

- Spend less time learning and more time coding with practical eBooks and Videos from over 4,000 industry professionals

- Improve your learning with Skill Plans built especially for you

- Get a free eBook or video every month

- Mapt is fully searchable

- Copy and paste, print, and bookmark content

PacktPub.com

Did you know that Packt offers eBook versions of every book published, with PDF and ePub files available? You can upgrade to the eBook version at `www.PacktPub.com` and as a print book customer, you are entitled to a discount on the eBook copy. Get in touch with us at `service@packtpub.com` for more details.

At `www.PacktPub.com`, you can also read a collection of free technical articles, sign up for a range of free newsletters, and receive exclusive discounts and offers on Packt books and eBooks.

Foreword

Twenty years ago, the world was introduced to a bright yellow LEGO brick made of more than just plastic. Powered by 6 AA batteries, the simple 3-input 3-output RCX was born. With this brick, the LEGO Group launched LEGO MINDSTORMS, a new brand to combine robotics with the iconic LEGO platform. Like millions of other children over the past two decades, this combination of building and programming would launch my career.

The modern LEGO MINDSTORMS EV3 continues to inspire children. However, like any new technology, getting started can be difficult. Kyle, or as I will forever know him, Builderdude35, is a great friend, and cornerstone of the modern LEGO MINDSTORMS community. For years, Kyle has introduced both children and adults to LEGO MINDSTORMS via his YouTube channel. In this book, Kyle takes some of the outstanding lessons and formulates tutorials to aid both the novice and advanced users, alike. From introducing the use of real-world data through sensors to programming GPS-based navigation, this book features a unique set of projects for any aspiring roboticist.

Besides providing a starting point with LEGO MINDSTORMS, Kyle showcases his own discoveries in creating the iconic Timmyton and Grunt robots. Focusing on human-robot interaction, these robots showcase how to make robotics inviting and provide character to an otherwise predictable machine. This book is another example of Kyle sharing his wisdom with the community and contributing to the rich LEGO MINDSTORMS legacy. Like Builderdude35's YouTube channel, may this book help you to discover something new, inspire others, and share in the MINDSTORMS magic!

Andy Milluzzi

LEGO MINDSTORMS Community Partner

Contributors

About the author

Kyle Markland is a young robotics enthusiast and aspiring engineer who is committed to helping others learn about technology. His first introduction to robotics was when he joined a FIRST LEGO League (FLL) team. In 2015, he started a weekly series of robotics tutorials on his YouTube channel `Builderdude35`. The videos aims to teach viewers engineering and programming concepts such as PID line following, dog gears, and pneumatics. In recognition of his efforts in robotics education, LEGO MINDSTORMS officially named Kyle a MINDSTORMS Community Partner (MCP) in August 2017.

I would like to thank my parents for their support and patience as I wrote this book, my biggest project yet. I am deeply indebted to Marc-André Bazergui not only for serving as my technical editor, but also for welcoming me into the online MINDSTORMS community. Thank you to Sharon Raj, Komal Karne, Rahul Nair, and the rest of the publication team for their hard work and for making my dream of becoming an author a reality.

About the reviewer

Marc-André Bazergui has been with IBM for over 20 years. He is currently a technical solution manager in the Power Systems team. His spare time is spent creating LEGO robots and sharing his passion for MINDSTORMS with the world. He has been a member of the MINDSTORMS Community Partner (MCP) program since 2009. This led him to be involved with the development of the EV3 in 2011. Among his contributions are the design for the EV3 robot, KRAZ3, one of the 12 bonus robots you can build with the LEGO MINDSTORMS 31313 kit. You can find more about Marc-André's work online under the pseudonym bazmarc.

Packt is searching for authors like you

If you're interested in becoming an author for Packt, please visit authors.packtpub.com and apply today. We have worked with thousands of developers and tech professionals, just like you, to help them share their insight with the global tech community. You can make a general application, apply for a specific hot topic that we are recruiting an author for, or submit your own idea.

Table of Contents

Preface

Building Smart LEGO MINDSTORMS EV3 Robots explores six EV3 projects that range from a low intermediate level to an advanced level. Each chapter uses examples to teach the building and programming concepts applied in each project, then relating them to an application in a real-world smart robot. Each chapter builds on the knowledge learned in the previous chapter, which makes a structured progression that expands your library of EV3 knowledge as you work your way up to the most advanced project in the final chapter. By the time you finish the book, you will have achieved mastery of EV3 and will have developed all of the skills necessary to make your own EV3 robots.

LEGO MINDSTORMS EV3 is a fantastic robotics platform for enthusiasts of all ages and skill levels. Since its inception, MINDSTORMS has made robotics accessible for an entire generation of hobbyists. EV3 is the third iteration of LEGO MINDSTORMS robotics, and it has provided an introduction to robotics for many young enthusiasts. Robots are assembled using the versatile LEGO Technic elements and are animated using motors. Sensors enable the robots to respond to the environment. Finally, programs are written on a computer using unique graphical software and downloaded to the EV3 intelligent brick to make the robot come to life. EV3 has become a staple in classrooms, homes, and in the FIRST LEGO League robotics competition as educators worldwide have recognized its educational value. The EV3 has proven itself to be a tool for serious learning while delivering the fun of playing with LEGO.

Who this book is for

This book is for anyone who is interested in getting started with robotics and wants to learn building and programming concepts so that they can start making their own robots. Readers should be familiar with the basics of using EV3 and its graphical programming and have experience with the LEGO Technic building system.

What this book covers

Chapter 1, *Introduction to Smart Robots*, explains what qualities a robot must have in order to be considered smart and discusses two examples of smart robots in the real world. Then, it introduces the LEGO MINDSTORMS EV3 robotics platform and summarizes the six projects included in this book.

Chapter 2, *Security Tank – Object-Tracking Robot*, explains how tank-style driving works; introduces mechanisms such as gear ratios, turntables, cams, and EV3's infrared sensor; explores the advantages of using proportional logic in a smart robot, and outlines how to make a beacon following program that applies proportional logic.

Chapter 3, *Omnilander – Ultimate All-Terrain Vehicle*, reapplies tank tracks for a rugged off-road application; introduces advanced mechanisms such as the worm gear, rack-and-pinion gears, and clutches; describes how to make a remote control program for a tank-style robot; and explains how to use proximity sensors to make an autonomous collision avoidance program.

Chapter 4, *Timmyton – Interactive Robotic Shark*, covers the original one-kit-wonder's compact mechanical design, its innovative custom GUI that incorporates several programs into one, programming the color sensor, and the myriad of programming features that make this robotic shark come to life.

Chapter 5, *Grunt - Quirky Bipedal Robot*, demonstrates a simple walking mechanism that can be used in an EV3 project, shows how a robot's cosmetic design can develop its personality, describes how nested switches can enable a robot to make decision making, and lists the programming features that lend Grunt its rich interactive qualities.

Chapter 6, *Falcon - Remote Control Race Car*, explains how to build a drivetrain and steering system that are modeled after those found in a real-world car, shows how to program car-style steering that automatically returns to the center, describes how to create a remote control program for a car-style robot, and introduces the basics of MyBlocks.

Chapter 7, *GPS Car - Autonomous EV3 Navigation*, introduces two navigation sensors (the GPS receiver and the magnetic compass) and outlines the basic knowledge necessary for using them. Then, it describes how to modify the Falcon to incorporate these sensors and explains how to program the car to use the sensors to autonomously navigate to a pair of GPS coordinates defined by the user.

To get the most out of this book

- Install EV3 Home Edition (version 1.2.2 or newer) on your computer. The software can be downloaded from `https://www.lego.com/en-us/mindstorms/downloads/download-software`.
- Spend some time familiarizing yourself with EV3. It is graphical programming software in which programs are written by connecting code blocks together. You should know the names of the blocks and where to find each one of them in the programming palette. You should also be comfortable with dragging and dropping blocks to place them in your program, know how to change their modes, and have a basic understanding of what individual blocks do.
- Familiarize yourself with the EV3 brick and understand the basics of using it. Know how to power it on and off, download programs from a computer via the USB cable, navigate its menus to select a program to run, and replace the batteries when necessary.
- You should have experience of building with LEGO Technic. All of the robots in this book are made using Technic elements.
- You may choose to install LEGO Digital Designer (LDD) version 4.3 on your computer. You can download the LDD software from `https://www.lego.com/en-us/ldd/download`. LDD is a LEGO CAD program that allows you to build and view digital models of LEGO creations. It also allows you to generate building instructions for a digital model. The LDD software will guide you when you build the projects in this book. You can download the LDD files (`.lxf`) for each project from `http://builderdude35.com/downloads-2/` and open them using the LDD software.
- In addition to an EV3 retail set (31313), you will need additional LEGO Technic elements for the projects included in this book. (The only exception is the Timmyton, which can be made with the parts included in one EV3 retail set). You can use LDD to generate a bill of materials, which will help you identify the additional Technic elements you will need. `Chapter 7`, *GPS Car – Autonomous EV3 Navigation*, also requires some third-party hardware from Dexter Industries and HiTechnic.
- Before you start programming, update the firmware on your EV3 brick to version 1.09H or newer. Perform the following steps to update your EV3 brick's firmware:
  1. Start EV3 Home Edition on your computer.
  2. Turn on your EV3 brick and plug it into your computer using a USB cable.
  3. Open a new project in EV3.

4. Navigate to **Tools** | **Firmware Update**.
5. If version 1.09H is not already available, follow the steps to download it from `https://www.lego.com/en-us/mindstorms/`.
6. Select the firmware version 1.09H (or newer, if available), click on **Update Firmware**, and wait for the update to complete. The EV3 brick will restart when the update is complete.

Download the example code files

You can download the example code files for this book from your account at `www.packtpub.com`. If you purchased this book elsewhere, you can visit `www.packtpub.com/support` and register to have the files emailed directly to you.

You can download the code files by following these steps:

1. Log in or register at `www.packtpub.com`.
2. Select the **SUPPORT** tab.
3. Click on **Code Downloads & Errata**.
4. Enter the name of the book in the **Search** box and follow the onscreen instructions.

Once the file is downloaded, please make sure that you unzip or extract the folder using the latest version of:

- WinRAR/7-Zip for Windows
- Zipeg/iZip/UnRarX for Mac
- 7-Zip/PeaZip for Linux

The code bundle for the book is also hosted on GitHub at `https://github.com/PacktPublishing/Building-Smart-LEGO-MINDSTORMS-EV3-Robots`. In case there's an update to the code, it will be updated on the existing GitHub repository.

We also have other code bundles from our rich catalog of books and videos available at `https://github.com/PacktPublishing/`. Check them out!

Download the color images

We also provide a PDF file that has color images of the screenshots/diagrams used in this book. You can download it here: https://www.packtpub.com/sites/default/files/downloads/BuildingSmartLEGOMINDSTORMSEV3Robots_ColorImages.pdf.

Robots in action

Visit the following link to check out the robots in action:

https://goo.gl/GB4sFr

Conventions used

There are a number of text conventions used throughout this book.

CodeInText: Indicates code words in text, database table names, folder names, filenames, file extensions, pathnames, dummy URLs, user input, and Twitter handles. Here is an example: "Set the target number of degrees to 600; this is how far the motor needs to rotate to fire two projectiles."

Bold: Indicates a new term, an important word, or words that you see onscreen. For example, words in menus or dialog boxes appear in the text like this. Here is an example: "The mode on the switch block should be set to **Motor Rotation** | **Compare** | **Degrees**."

 Warnings or important notes appear like this.

 Tips and tricks appear like this.

Get in touch

Feedback from our readers is always welcome.

General feedback: Email `feedback@packtpub.com` and mention the book title in the subject of your message. If you have questions about any aspect of this book, please email us at `questions@packtpub.com`.

Errata: Although we have taken every care to ensure the accuracy of our content, mistakes do happen. If you have found a mistake in this book, we would be grateful if you would report this to us. Please visit `www.packtpub.com/submit-errata`, selecting your book, clicking on the Errata Submission Form link, and entering the details.

Piracy: If you come across any illegal copies of our works in any form on the Internet, we would be grateful if you would provide us with the location address or website name. Please contact us at `copyright@packtpub.com` with a link to the material.

If you are interested in becoming an author: If there is a topic that you have expertise in and you are interested in either writing or contributing to a book, please visit `authors.packtpub.com`.

Reviews

Please leave a review. Once you have read and used this book, why not leave a review on the site that you purchased it from? Potential readers can then see and use your unbiased opinion to make purchase decisions, we at Packt can understand what you think about our products, and our authors can see your feedback on their book. Thank you!

For more information about Packt, please visit `packtpub.com`.

Introduction to Smart Robots 1

What are smart robots? At today's pace of technological innovation, the word *smart* is being applied to all sorts of devices: smartphones, smart watches, smart televisions, and the list goes on. The word is even in the title of this book! But what does it mean when we say that a robot is smart? What do smart robots do, and how do they accomplish their task?

What makes a robot smart?

When we talk about smart robots, we are not necessarily referring to an advanced artificial intelligence like those in a science fiction movie or a supercomputer that wins the Jeopardy championship, although those are some *very smart* robots. The definition of a smart robot is actually much broader and includes some devices you may not have originally considered smart.

A smart robot is simply any device that uses sensors to measure some condition in its environment, then decides what to do next based on a set of pre-programmed instructions. They have some kind of computer or controller acting as their *brain* that processes the sensor information and interprets these instructions. You can think of the software loaded into the robot as the set of instructions that the smart robot follows. The software's programming allows a smart robot to make an observation, then make a decision based on this observation. Of course, a person must first build the robot and write the software, but after that, a smart robot operates on its own without human intervention.

To put it more concisely, a smart robot is a machine that does all of the following things or has all of the following features:

- It is able to follow a series of pre-programmed instructions specified by the user or engineer
- It is able to makes an observation about the outside world

- It has a central computer or other type of controller that interprets both the instructions in the software and the data from the sensor
- It is able to make a decision and react based on the observation, following the instructions defined in the program
- It is able to complete all of the preceding steps automatically, without human intervention

The ability to make a decision on its own without help from a person is what makes a robot smart. The more decisions a robot can make on its own, the smarter it is.

As you can see, this definition still includes the obvious examples of smart robots that we discussed earlier, but it also includes some simpler devices. Using this definition, a robotic vacuum cleaner is considered a smart robot!

Examples of smart robots in the real world

That definition may have seemed somewhat abstract, so let's put it into context with two real-world examples. We will first discuss a simple smart robot—the robotic vacuum cleaner—then talk about a much more sophisticated example—the autonomous car.

Robotic vacuum cleaners

These are some of the simpler smart robots that you are likely to encounter, but they are nonetheless smart robots because they fulfill all of the points of our definition:

- **They follow a series of pre-programmed instructions**: These machines come with their vacuum-cleaning program pre-installed on their control unit. The engineers who developed the product have already sorted out what the robot needs to do during its routine to keep the floors clean. The software is installed on each robot before it leaves the factory. After the customer purchases the robot, all they have to do is charge it, then turn it on, and it gets right to work, following the instructions that the engineers defined in the software.

- **They make an observation about the outside world**: The vacuum robot has some sensors that allow it to make observations about where it is in the room. On the front of the robot, there is a bumper equipped with an impact sensor. When the robot collides with the wall, the impact sensor is pressed, and the robot knows it has reached the end of the room:

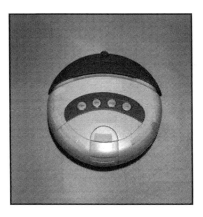

The user can also set up an invisible *fence* using infrared emitters that confine the robot to one area. The robot is equipped with an infrared sensor that can detect this fence and tell the robot that it has reached the end of the area to be cleaned.

Infrared refers to a type of light that is invisible to humans. Robots can be equipped with specialized sensors that detect infrared light. This makes for a convenient way to set a barrier for a robot that will not obstruct a human, as people cannot see or touch infrared light.

Finally, the robot's charging pad has an infrared beacon. When the job is complete, the robot uses its infrared sensor to navigate back to the charging pad to replenish its battery:

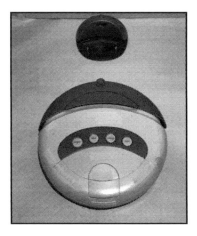

- **They have a central computer/controller that interprets instructions and sensor data**: The robotic vacuum has a central controller that runs the software set at the factory and receives input form the robot's impact and infrared sensors. Though this central controller is not necessarily a powerful supercomputer, it has the ability to interpret the software and sensor measurements to decide what to do next.

- **They make a decision and react based on the observation, following the instructions defined in the program**: The robot proceeds during its cleaning routine as the software specifies. The sensors tell the robot when it needs to change its course; if the impact sensor detects that the robot has collided with a physical wall, or the infrared sensor detects an invisible wall, the robot knows that it has come to the end of the area it is supposed to clean. It reacts by turning and moving in a different direction. The robot decides to alter its course based on the measurements from its sensors.

- **They complete all of these steps automatically**: The robot does everything without the help of a person; it cleans the floor while staying within the bounds of its room and returns itself to its base to recharge when it is finished. The only human assistance it needs is when the vacuum bag needs to be replaced.

Autonomous cars

Autonomous (also known as self-driving) cars are a much more sophisticated type of smart robot, yet they still fulfill the criteria we defined earlier:

- **They follow a series of pre-programmed instructions**: The engineers develop advanced software that enables the car to drive itself. They program all of the conditions necessary for driving so the car drives safely and follows the law, but the car is also programmed to learn as it drives!

- **They make an observation about the outside world**: Driving is a very complex task, especially for a robot, so a self-driving car needs to take in a large volume of information about its environment. A GPS receiver tells the vehicle where it is in the world. In addition, it needs to keep an eye or eyes on the road to avoid collision with objects, pedestrians, and other cars. An autonomous car may use an assortment of ultrasonic sensors; LIDAR, which is a light-based radar; machine vision; and more to monitor what is happening around it.

- **They have a central computer/controller that interprets instructions and sensor data**: An autonomous car has multiple computers that work together to processes the sensor data, run the software, and manage the car's responses to the road. Because there is a large amount of information to manage and reactions need to be made within fractions of a second, these computers need to be very powerful.

- **They make a decision and react based on the observation, following the instructions defined in the program**: The GPS receiver tells the car what road it is currently traveling on and where its destination is in relation to its current position. The self-driving car reacts by making the proper turns to get to the destination. The proximity and vision sensors help keep the car safe. If an object is detected in the road, the vehicle either stops or maneuvers to avoid it. If the car's vision system sees a stop sign or a red light, the vehicle makes the appropriate stop. If the lane sensors detect that the car is nearing the edge of the lane, the car responds by steering itself back into the center of the lane. If the proximity sensors detect that the vehicle is too close to the car in front of it, the self-driving car slows down to maintain a safe distance in-between itself and the other vehicle. The sensors provide the car with the information it needs to regulate its driving. The computers then decide what the best course of action is based on the information. The result is an autonomous car that reaches its destination safely.

- **They complete all of these steps automatically**: A self-driving car follows all of the rules of the road and reaches its destination without the need for any driver input. After all, the purpose of such a vehicle is to be able to navigate on its own! Because of the large volume of information it processes and the amount of decisions it needs to make to complete its task, an autonomous car is a very smart robot!

Where does the EV3 fit in?

In this book, we will be using the LEGO MINDSTORMS EV3 to make our own smart robots. The EV3 is ideal for building smart robots at this level for several reasons:

- It allows robotics enthusiasts of all skill levels to quickly prototype their own robots.
- It includes a suite of cool sensors that our robot can use to gather information about its environment.

- It has its own unique, intuitive programming language and development environment that allow us to write programs to control our smart robot.
- It includes motors and other hardware that enable it to interact with its environment.
- The EV3 intelligent brick acts as the *brain* of the robot. It runs the program, processes information from the sensors, makes decisions, and controls the motors.

The EV3 robotics platform is convenient, accessible, and includes everything that we need to build our own smart robots.

What will we build and why?

This book will walk you through six different projects:

- Security Tank, which uses an infrared sensor to follow a beacon and aim its turret. This robot demonstrates the use of infrared technology for tracking a beacon, as well using proportional logic for a smooth feedback system.
- Omnilander, which can climb up steep slopes using its heavy-duty tank tracks. Special hardware gives it the ability to scale vertical obstacles. This project demonstrates the effectiveness of tracks for all-terrain navigation and shows specialized mechanisms, such as worm gears, rack-and-pinion, and clutches in action.
- Timmyton, an interactive robotic shark that features a custom GUI that allows the user to select multiple programs from within one main program. This project demonstrates features that can be incorporated into a robot to create a fun interactive experience. It also shows how computers use a GUI to allow the user to navigate between different programs through a more user-friendly interface.
- Grunt, a quirky bipedal robot with a mind of his own! This robot uses an array of sensors to detect and react to nearby people. This project demonstrates how nested programming switches can enable a robot to have smooth, lifelike decision making and create a rich interactive experience. Special programming and careful visual design give this whimsical creation a unique personality.
- Falcon, a fast race car that is controlled using the infrared remote and receiver. It showcases some of the mechanical concepts that are at work in real-world cars and features an intelligent return-to-center steering program.

- GPS car, which incorporates a GPS receiver and a digital magnetic compass. The user can input coordinates, and this robot will navigate to the destination. This project demonstrates the principles of GPS navigation and shows how GPS helps an autonomous car in the real world get to where it needs to go.

Each of these EV3 robots is a small-scale smart machine that demonstrates concepts that are applicable to a real-world smart robot. As you complete the projects, you will not only learn about the robots themselves but also about how smart robots are built and programmed in the real world. You will learn about the engineering concepts that work behind the scenes to allow these robots to complete their tasks.

Summary

Let's quickly recap what we have learned in this chapter.

We learned that a smart robot is any robot that incorporates some level of intelligence in the form of autonomous decision making. A smart robot uses sensors to make an observation about the outside world, then makes a decision based on an observation according to its programming.

We applied our definition of a smart robot to two real-world examples: a robotic vacuum cleaner and an autonomous car. We discussed the ways in which both fulfill each of the criteria for consideration as a smart robot.

We discussed why we will use the EV3 robotics platform for prototyping the smart robotic projects in this book.

Finally, we listed the six projects that are included in this book. We talked about the cool things each of these robots can do and how they help us understand smart robots in the real world.

In the next chapter, we will dive into our first project, the Security Tank!

2
Security Tank – Object-Tracking Robot

It is time to tackle our first project! In this chapter, we will build and program a small EV3 tank that uses infrared sensors to track and target a beacon. You can think of it as a miniature model tank that you can use to keep your room safe from intruders!

The tank demonstrates how smart robots in the real world use infrared technology. We briefly mentioned this technology in the first chapter. Infrared refers to a wavelength of light that is invisible to the human eye. However, robots can incorporate sensors that can detect infrared light. This makes infrared a convenient way to invisibly send messages to a robot or allow a robot to see something that a human cannot see.

The EV3 remote control can serve as a beacon that continuously emits an infrared signal. The tank we will be building in this chapter is equipped with two EV3 infrared sensors. The sensors measure the heading and distance of the infrared beacon. Using this information, the robot can aim its turret at the beacon but also steer itself to keep the beacon within its line of sight.

The tank we build in this chapter also demonstrates some mechanical concepts often found in smart robots. In addition to infrared beacon tracking, you will learn about caterpillar tracks, turntables, cams, and gear reduction.

 You can download the LDD file for this project at http://builderdude35. com/ on the **Downloads** page. This is a LEGO CAD file that is opened with the LEGO Digital Designer program, which is a free download. When you open the file with the program, you can view a 3D model of the project and generate building instructions and a bill of materials.

Now, let's get to the project and make a tank:

Technical requirements

You must have EV3 Home Edition Software V1.2.2 or newer installed on your computer. You may also install LEGO Digital Designer (LDD) V4.3 and download the LDD file for this project to guide you in the building process.

The LDD file is available on the **Downloads** page of the the Builderdude35 website:

http://builderdude35.com/download/security-tank-ldd/

The LDD and EV3 files for this chapter are available on GitHub:

```
https://github.com/PacktPublishing/Building-Smart-LEGO-MINDSTORMS-EV3-Robots/
tree/master/Chapter02
```

Check out this video to see the robot in action:

```
https://goo.gl/Ws526r
```

Mechanical design

First, we will be taking a look at each of the mechanisms that allow the Security Tank to do its job.

Drivetrain

The drivetrain is the mechanical system that allows a robot to move. The drivetrain on the Security Tank is actually quite simple. It uses caterpillar tracks, also known as **tank treads**.

Tank treads consist of a belt or a chain that runs across at least two wheels or pulleys. They work in pairs, with one on each side of the vehicle. The treads essentially make two large, continuous surfaces that the robot drives on. This provides a large contact area with the ground and allows a tank to have maximum traction over all surfaces. Changing the power split between the left and right tracks allows the robot to steer. This is what the term **tank steering** refers to.

As you might have guessed, our Security Tank is equipped with two caterpillar tracks and has tank-style steering. One EV3 large motor drives each of the tracks; the left EV3 large motor is plugged into motor port B and drives the left caterpillar track, and the right EV3 large motor is plugged into port C and drives the right track.

There is no gearing between the EV3 motors and the tracks. Rather, the motors directly drive their respective tracks. This makes for a compact, robust, simple drive system. The downside is that the tank drives slowly. But this project is not about building a speed machine; that is something we will cover later in this book.

When you take a look at the underside of the robot, you can see both of the drive motors, each paired with a tank tread:

There are two more things you should notice: the first is that the EV3 brick is mounted on the bottom of the robot, between the two drive motors, facing downward towards the ground. The brick actually acts as a structural part of the chassis. Placing the EV3 brick here helps to make the tank very compact. However, the downside is that it is not conveniently located; the user will need to lift the robot to access the brick and switch the programs. This is an example of a trade-off you may face when engineering your own robots, and you will need to ask yourself which is more important for the specific robot you are building: accomplishing a mechanical goal, or maintaining ease of use (ergonomics) for the user. For this project, ease of use is sacrificed to make a neater, more compact robot.

The second thing that you may have noticed is that there is a small pulley attached to the right drive motor. This pulley drives a rubber band that runs around the spiked roller in the front of the tank. This system is set up so that when the tank drives, the spiked roller will turn as well. This is an example of a clever way in which you can accomplish more than one task with one motor!

Turret

The turret consists of two small cannons mounted on top of the tank. The turret can swivel back and forth to aim at the infrared beacon and fire LEGO spheres as projectiles. It is powered by two EV3 medium motors:

Let's take a closer look at how each part of the turret works!

Firing projectiles

Two cannons on top of the tank fire LEGO spheres. They are made of the special LEGO element that is specifically designed for this purpose. Both cannons are powered by the same EV3 medium motor, which is plugged into port A.

The motor splits its power to both cannons through a 90-degree gear connection. On either side there is a cam mechanism. When the motor spins, the cams slide a rod back and forth through the firing element. When the cam pushes the rod into the forward position, it ejects a sphere from the firing element at high velocity. This is how the turret *fires* the spheres. The motor continues to rotate the cam, and the rod slides back to make room for another sphere, which reloads the cannon. By simply setting the motor to spin continuously in one direction, each cannon can automatically fire a sphere, reload, then repeat the process:

The two cannons operate simultaneously, but their cams are staggered 180 degrees, which causes them to alternate their firing. This is done for two reasons: the first is that this allows the firing to be smoother because one cannon will reload while the other is firing. The second reason is to balance the load on the motor. The motor needs to apply force to fire a projectile, so opposing the cams evens out the load and makes it more manageable for the motor.

The gear ratio on the 90-degree connection is 1.67:1, meaning that it takes 1.67 turns of the motor to cycle the cams once. Aside from slowing the rotation, this increases the torque that the motor applies to the spheres and further decreases the load on the motor.

 Gear ratios are essential to mechanical engineering and can alter the speed and torque of a mechanism. Here, gear ratios are used to increase the torque the motor can apply and helps the motor fire the projectiles. We will explore gear ratios in more detail in the next chapter when we build the Omnilander.

Here is the turret mechanism; the ammo silos have been removed to give us a clearer view:

Ammo silos

Above each of the cannons sits a tall ammo silo that holds additional spheres. Each silo holds up to seven spheres, for a total capacity of 14. The silos reload the cannons after they have fired a projectile. They are gravity powered; after a sphere is launched, another one drops down into the cannon to fill its place:

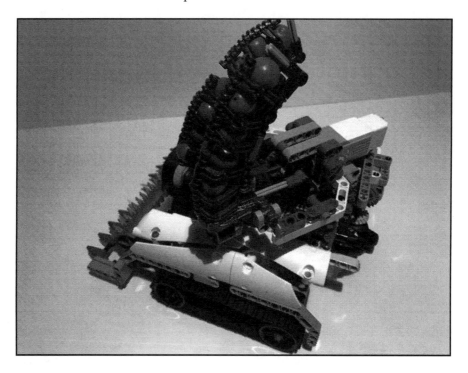

Though the ammo silos are a necessary part of the design, they are quite ugly. This is another example of an engineering trade-off you may encounter when designing your own smart robot—functionality versus cosmetic design. Sometimes it is difficult to make a beautiful robot that also does exactly what you want it to do.

Rotation

The tank also needs to be able to aim at the beacon. The entire turret assembly is mounted on a turntable, which allows it to rotate to the right and left. The turntable is powered by an EV3 medium motor, which is plugged into port D:

This motor is located in the back of the robot to the right side. It sends its power through a 90-degree gear connection, which is very similar to the one used with the cannons. However, there is another set of gears in this mechanism: a 24-tooth gear drives the gear on the turntable mechanism. The overall gear ratio between the motor and the turntable is 4.17:1, meaning the motor must make 4.17 rotations to get the turret to rotate a full 360 degrees. This is a much slower gear ratio than the one we saw on the cannon. Slowing down the rotation of the turret makes its motion more accurate and easier to control:

Spiked roller

This is an extra flourish added to the tank to improve its visual impact! This does not have a specific mechanical function, but it makes the tank look awesome:

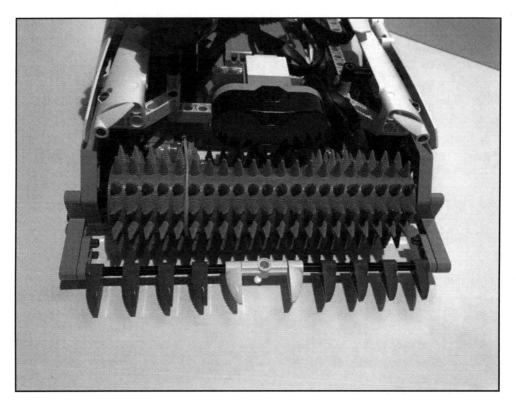

The large, spiked roller on the front of the tank adds to its menacing appearance. Earlier in the chapter, we discussed how the roller is set up with a pulley and a rubber band that are attached to one of the drive motors, which makes the roller spin when the tank drives.

The roller is a custom 3D-printed part. You can download the file for the roller where you downloaded the LDD for the tank earlier:

If you do not have the means necessary to 3D print this component, or you would rather use only true LEGO elements in your project, you can replace the 3D-printed spiked roller with another roller design that uses the large LEGO wheel hubs:

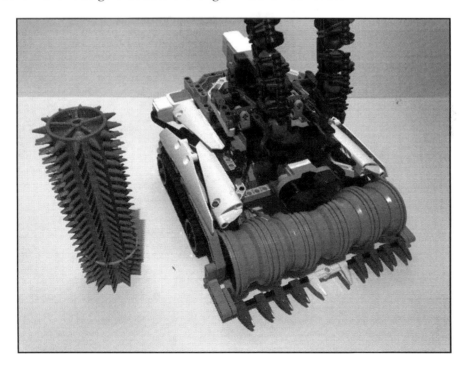

The roller adds an extra dimension to the tank's design and contributes to the overall cool factor. When you design your own smart robots, you should think about extra features to add to your project that may not serve a functional purpose, but rather contribute to the appearance of the robot. These types of additions show that you have gone the extra mile to make your robot more impressive.

Sensors

The tank uses two EV3 **infrared** (**IR**) sensors to measure information about the beacon's position:

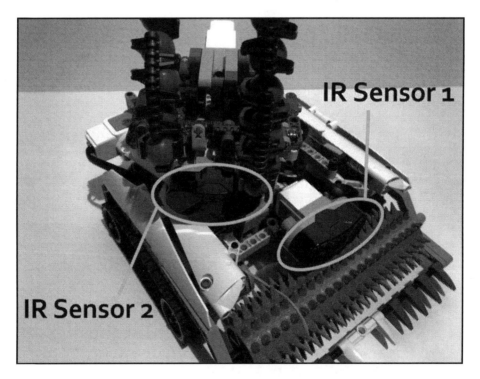

The first IR sensor is fixed to the tank's chassis and is plugged into sensor port 1. This sensor measures the beacon's heading and distance and adjusts the speed and steering of the tank's driving.

The second IR sensor is plugged into port 2. This sensor is mounted to the turret; it rotates along with the turret and follows the beacon. This sensor also measures the beacon's heading, but, instead of controlling the tank's steering, it controls the angle of the turret.

In the next section, you will learn more about each senor's specific responsibilities and how to program each one to make a cohesive smart robot!

Programming

Now we need to write a program that makes this smart tank move. We will be using EV3-G, the graphical programming language designed for the EV3.

Setting up the program

Before we start to write the program, we need to assign port numbers to both of the IR sensors. The program makes use of both of the IR sensors on the robot. The IR sensor that is mounted to the robot's chassis is plugged into port 1, so we will refer to this sensor as *IR 1*. The sensor mounted to the turret is plugged into port 2, so we will refer to that sensor as *IR 2*. It is imperative to remember this because the program identifies these sensors using their port numbers. We use the port numbers to tell the robot which sensor to check at any given time.

Now that we have established the numbers we will use to identify the sensors, we can start writing the program!

The first block we will add into our program is a loop block. By default, its condition will be set to repeat infinitely. Since that is what we want, there is no need to change it! This will serve as the master loop; the rest of the robot's programming will go inside this loop. It makes the program repeat indefinitely until the user manually stops it using the button on the EV3 brick:

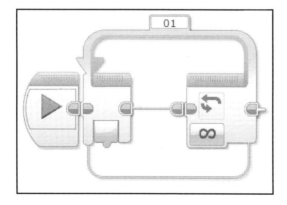

Beacon check

Before the robot starts to move, it needs to check to see that a beacon is present. We are going to start programming inside of our master loop, and the first part of the program inside of the loop will be a switch that checks to see if there is a nearby beacon. That way, the robot will not try to find and follow a beacon if none are present.

Setting up the switch

At the heart of the beacon check-step is a switch block. The program reads IR 2 to see whether a beacon is nearby. Then, based on the result, the robot will execute one of two cases.

Drag out an IR sensor block and insert it inside of the loop. Set the sensor block's mode (in the bottom-left corner of the block) to **Measure | Beacon**. The channel number of the beacon that the program will look for is set to channel 1 by default. There is no need to change this unless you want the program to work on a different channel. Whichever channel you choose, make sure that the channel chosen in the program matches the channel selected on the remote control.

Next, drag out a switch block and place it after the IR sensor block. By default, the switch block will read a touch sensor and determine which case to execute based on that sensor's current state. Change the switch's mode to *logic*. Now the switch will assign one case a *true* value and the other a *false* value, and the input to the switch block will determine which of the cases runs.

We will now connect the sensor block to the switch so that if there is a nearby beacon, the sensor block returns a value of *true* and the switch executes its top *true* case. If there is no beacon present, the block will return a *false* value and the switch will execute its bottom *false* case. To do this, simply find the *detected* output of the sensor block (the last output on the block) and drag a data wire from this output into the input of the logic switch.

Note that the data wire is a green/teal color. This indicates that this data wire handles logic data, or values of *true* and *false*.

When you finish each of these steps, your program should look like this:

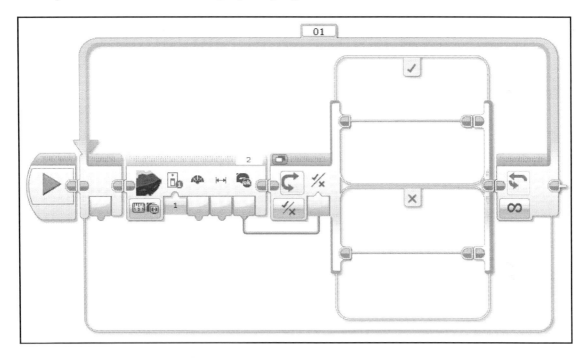

Programming the false case

We can now write some programming inside of the switch. We will start with the *false* case because it is simpler. This case will run if IR 2 does not see a beacon. If there is no nearby beacon, we simply want the robot to stop and wait until one is present.

Add three motor blocks into the bottom case of the switch. Each of these will stop the corresponding motor. The first block is a medium motor block. Set its mode to **Off** and set its port to A. This will halt the medium motor in port A, which controls the firing of the turret.

The second motor block will be a move tank block, which simultaneously controls the two drive motors. Set the mode of this block to **Off** as well. This will stop the robot's driving if no beacon is present. By default, the block controls the EV3 large motors in port B + C. These ports are correct, so there is no need to change it.

Add one more medium motor block with its mode set to **Off**. This time, be sure to set this block to port D. This will stop the turret from pivoting if no beacon is present.

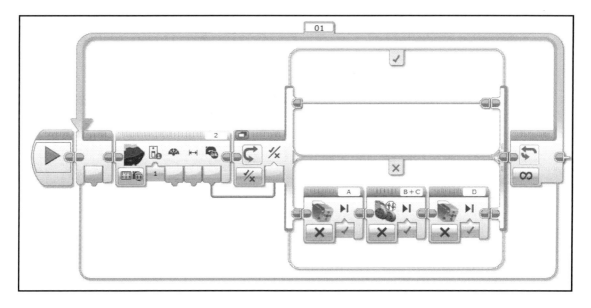

Change to tabbed view

In the top left corner of the switch block, there is a small button that toggles **Tabbed View**. This compresses the switch slightly so that it only shows one case at a time, and you can switch between the two cases using the tabs at the top of the switch. We will be writing a lot of programming in the true case of the switch, so selecting tabbed view will streamline the program a bit.

 Tabbed view does not make any functional change to the program. It is simply for the convenience of the programmer, as it makes the program appear neater and makes it easier to navigate.

After selecting tabbed view, the switch will reconfigure itself and the code will look like this:

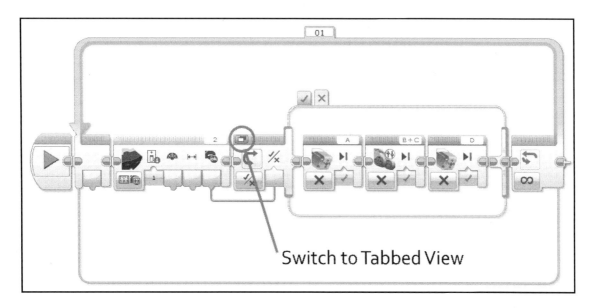

Switch to Tabbed View

We have finished the *false* case of the switch! The robot will check IR 2 to see whether a beacon is present. If there are no nearby beacons, the robot will halt all of its motors and wait until one comes within sight. But what if there is a beacon present?

Use the tabs at the top of the switch to select the *true* case. It is now time to start programming the *true* case:

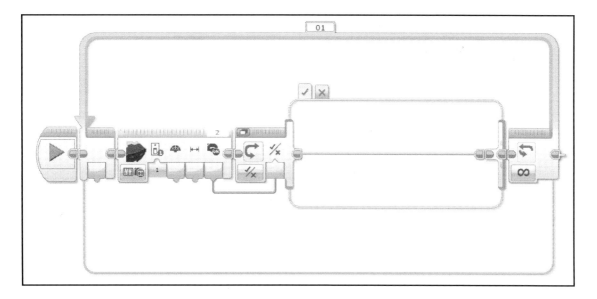

Following the beacon

The robot needs to steer itself while it follows the beacon. IR 1 will read the heading of the nearby beacon, and the robot will use the heading value to adjust its steering to keep itself on track with the beacon. IR 1 will also measure the distance to the beacon so that it can slow down when the beacon gets closer.

Add another IR sensor block and set its mode to **Measure | Beacon**. This time, make sure that the sensor port is set to 1. We will be using the first two outputs of this block: *heading* and *proximity*.

Proportional steering

The EV3 infrared sensor measures a beacon heading value from −25 to +25. A heading value of 0 indicates that the beacon is directly in front of the sensor. A positive value indicates that the beacon is to the right of the sensor, and a negative value indicates that the beacon is to the left. The magnitude of the heading value indicates how far the beacon is from the center. For example, a heading value of 5 means that the beacon is slightly to the right of the sensor, while a value of 23 would indicate that the beacon is far to the right of the sensor. The program will use both direction and magnitude to adjust its steering. This is called a proportional beacon follower, and it enables the robot to make smooth driving adjustments.

Proportional logic refers to a feedback loop in which the correction made by the system is proportional to the observed error. In our example, the tank will make a sharper turn if the beacon is farther away from the center of its vision. Here, proportional logic is applied to our beacon following program. Later in this book, we will apply it in other ways.

Measuring distance to control speed

The EV3 IR sensor can also provide a rough distance estimate for the beacon by measuring the strength of the signal it receives from the beacon. This can be accessed by using the *proximity* output on the IR sensor block. This distance figure is not expressed in centimeters or inches but rather serves as a relative distance figure. It is not perfectly accurate, either. However, we can still make use of this by making the tank slow down when the beacon gets near.

K values

We could use the heading and distance values measured by IR 1 to directly control the steering for the tank. However, this is not ideal. Instead, we need to multiply each of these values in order to scale them so that the resulting corrections fit better with the possible range of the hardware. The factor by which a measurement is multiplied is called a *k* value.

Most proportional feedback loops use a *k* value. In this part of the program, we will use two: the first (k_1) will multiply the measured beacon heading to control the magnitude of the steering, and the other (k_2) will multiply the measured distance to control the speed.

The optimal value for k_1 is 5. The optimal value for k_2 is 10. k_2 is set so that for any distance value greater than 10, the resulting power level of the drive motors will be greater than 100%. Not to worry, because the EV3 will simply run the motors at 100% power whenever it sees a value that is larger. k_2 is set this way because the tank should only slow down if the beacon is very close; the tank will drive at full power to follow the beacon unless the distance to the beacon is less than 10.

K values are arbitrary numbers, meaning they can be adjusted to suit the wishes of the programmer or the constraints of the hardware. A larger *k* value will mean the robot makes larger corrections relative to the measured error; a smaller *k* value would mean the robot makes smaller adjustments. Try experimenting with different *k* values to modify the performance of the tank and see whether you prefer a different *k* than the ones suggested here.

To incorporate these *k* values into the program, add a math block after the new sensor block and set its mode to *multiply*. Drag a data wire from the *heading* output of the sensor block and plug it into the input *a* of the math block. In the *b* input, enter a value of 5, the value we set for k_1.

These data wires are yellow, which indicates that the data type is numerical. As the name implies, these data types deal with some kind of number value.

Take out a second math block and set its mode to *multiply* as well. Place it after the first multiplication block. Drag out a data wire from the *proximity* output of the IR sensor block and plug it into the *a* input of the math block. Enter 10, the value we set for k_2, into the *b* input of the math block.

Controlling the driving

We have set up the heading and proximity values with their respective *k* values. We can now use these values to control the driving of the tank.

Add a move steering block after the second math block that you just placed. By default, it will be set to control the drive motors in port B + C; this is correct, so we will not change the port assignment. We will need to change the mode of the motor block to **On**.

Drag a data wire from *result*, the output of the first math block (the one with the value of k_1) and plug it into the *steering* input of the move steering block. Plug the result of the second math block into the *power* input of the move steering block.

Now, the heading and proximity values measured by IR 1 can adjust the speed and steering angle of the tank and enable it to follow the beacon! You have completed your proportional beacon follower, and it should look something like this:

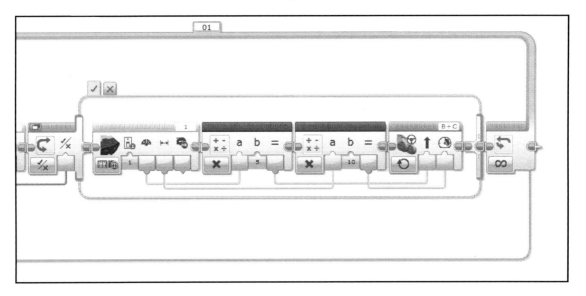

Aiming the turret

The robot will now use the second infrared sensor, IR 2, to aim the turret in the direction of the beacon. We will use proportional logic to control the aiming of the turret, just as we did for the driving. The heading value measured by IR 2 is multiplied by a *k* value and will set the target power for motor D, the motor responsible for rotating the turret.

We are going to start this new segment of programming directly after the proportional beacon follower we just wrote. Make sure the new code blocks are still within the switch block. Add a new infrared sensor block with its mode set to **Measure** | **Beacon**. This time, the port should be set to 2.

Add a math block set to *multiply* after the new IR sensor block. As before, this block will multiply the heading measurement from the IR sensor by a *k* value. The suggested *k* value for the turret turntable is 1.6.

 Although the *k* value for the turret (1.6) is smaller than the *k* value used for steering (5), the turntable responds faster than the steering. It is important to consider the mechanism attached to each motor when considering *k* values. Despite having a smaller *k* value, the turntable rotates faster because the hardware between it and the motor controlling it makes it respond more quickly than the steering on the drive motors.

The medium motor in port D controls the swivel of the turntable, so the third block to add is a medium motor block. Be sure to set the port to D and the mode to **On**.

Finally, plug the *heading* output from the sensor block into the *a* input of the math block. Then, plug the *result* of the math block into the *power* input of the medium motor block:

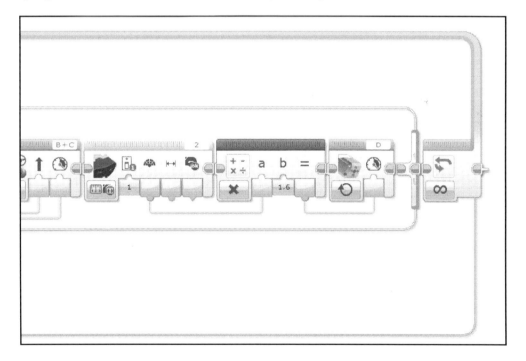

Now we have programmed the turret to swivel according to the heading value measured by IR 2 using a proportional algorithm.

Fire!

When the turret locks on to the beacon, the robot will fire two projectiles. The medium motor in port A controls the ball-launching mechanism. We will program the turret to fire based on the heading reading provided by IR 2. If the heading value is zero, then the turret is aimed directly at the beacon, and the robot can fire.

Using the compare switch

We will program a turret fire case directly after the aiming code we just wrote. Drag out a switch block and set its mode to **Infrared Sensor | Compare | Beacon Heading**. This mode allows us to set a desired beacon heading value. The EV3 will check the current sensor reading and compare it to the value we set here. The compare switch block is great because it combines three steps into a single block: it reads the sensor, compares its value to the desired target, then decides which case to execute based on whether the sensor value matches the target. In our specific example, if IR 2 measures a beacon heading of exactly zero, the EV3 will run the *true* case. Otherwise, it will run the *false* case.

We will set zero as our desired heading value; enter 0 into the *threshold value* input of the switch (the third input). We only want the turret to fire when the heading equals exactly zero, so the next step is to change the *compare type* (the second input on the switch block) to =. Finally, make sure that this switch block is using the sensor in port 2.

Program the switch cases

In the *true* case, we need to add the motor block to make the turret fire. We will add in a medium motor block and select port A. Then, change the mode to **On for Degrees**. Set the motor's power to 100%; the robot will need the full power of the motor to launch its projectiles. Set the target number of degrees to 600; this is how far the motor needs to rotate to fire two projectiles.

 If you find that the tank occasionally fires only one ball instead of two, you may need to increase the target number of degrees. This is because motor A is not rotating far enough to fire two projectiles each time. Conversely, if motor A rotates too far each time, you should decrease the target number of degrees.

What do we program in the *false* case? Well, nothing! We will leave this case empty because if the turret is not squarely aimed at the beacon, it should not launch any projectiles. So, we do not have to tell it to do anything!

Your completed fire case should look like this:

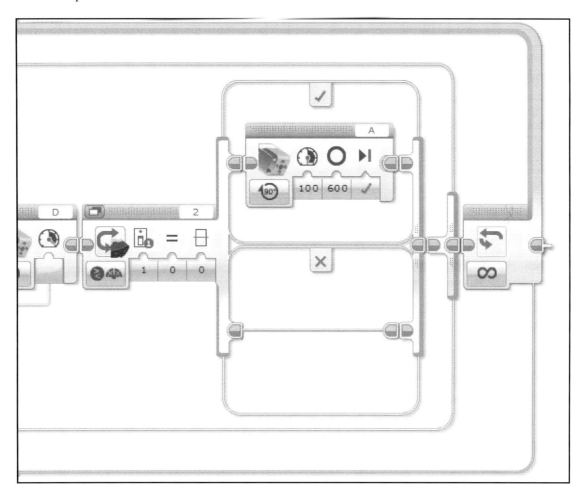

Keeping the beacon in sight

For the tank to follow the beacon, it is imperative that the tank keeps it within the range of its infrared sensor's sight at all times. Also, the turret on the tank can only rotate so far before it runs into its mechanical limit.

The final part of the program allows the tank to keep the beacon in sight while also preventing the turret from over-rotating. It will check to see if the turret has turned too far from the center; if it has, the tank will make a sharp turn to center the beacon in its field of view and reset the turret to a central position.

Set up the first switch (right side)

The program will check to see if the turret has swiveled too far away from the center. It will make use of the compare switch yet again, this time comparing the number of degrees on motor D to the threshold value that would indicate that it had rotated too far. The mode on the switch block should be set to **Motor Rotation | Compare | Degrees**.

When the turret swivels to the right of center, the degree count on motor D will be positive. When the turret swivels left, the degree count will be negative. Our robot will need to individually check to see if the turret is too far in each direction, so it will first check to see whether the turret is too far to the right. Therefore, this first switch will only be concerned with the positive direction. We will soon program a second switch that checks in the negative direction.

Set the compare type on the switch to > (type 2). The threshold value that we can say is too far is 250 degrees. Enter 250 into the second input of the switch:

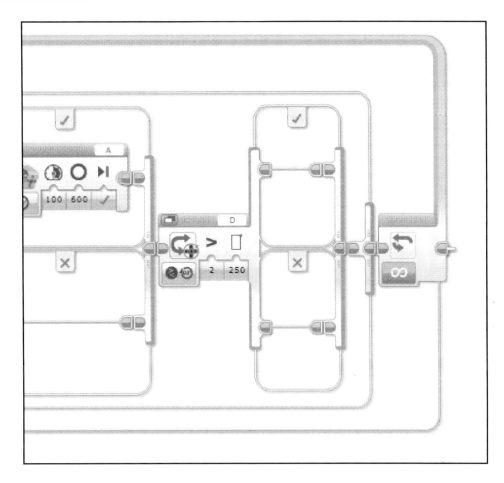

 Even though the maximum number of degrees we allow on motor D is 250, this only translates to just under 90 degrees of rotation on the turret. This is because of the gear reduction on the turret, which we discussed earlier in this chapter. One degree of rotation on motor D results in a fraction of a degree's worth of rotation on the turret.

This switch will check to see if motor D has rotated more than 250 degrees to the right of center. If this ends up being *true*, then the tank will need to make an adjustment to its steering and its turret. We will now program in the code that will make that adjustment.

Program the return-to-center (right side)

If the turret has strayed too far to the right (motor D has > | 250 degrees), the tank will need to make a sharp right turn to center the beacon within its line of sight again and center the turret. We will add some programming in the *true* case of our new switch that will do just that.

First, add a medium motor block and set it to turn motor D off. This case executes when the turret starts to rotate too far, so we need to stop it to make sure it does not over-rotate.

Next, the tank will make its sharp right turn. We will use the move tank block, which allows us to individually control the power of both drive motors (port B + C). Set its mode to **On for Seconds**. Set the power of motor B, the left drive motor, to 75 percent. Set the power of motor C, the right drive motor, to –75 percent. Powering the motors in opposite directions allows the tank to make a quick spin turn. We want the tank to turn for 1.2 seconds, so enter that as the target time value.

Directly after that, we can place another move tank block, this time with the mode set to **Off**. This will halt the drive motors after the tank has made its turn.

The last part of this segment is some code that returns the turret to center. Add a loop block. We will set a special exit case for this loop. Change the mode on the loop to **Motor Rotation | Compare | Degrees**. This will work in a similar manner to the compare switches we programmed earlier. We will set a target degree value and the motor will rotate until it reaches this target. Change the compare type to < (type 4) and make the threshold value 3 degrees. Make sure the motor in port D is selected. Inside the loop, place a medium motor block. Set the block to simply turn the motor **On** at –50 percent power. This loop will power motor D in the negative direction until its degree value is less than three (which is very close to the center):

It is good practice to set the target degree value to < 3 as opposed to = 0. This is because the EV3 motor encoders (also known as degree counters) have an error of about one degree; also, there are only so many times the EV3 can check the degree value on motor D in one second. As a result of these two factors, there is a very small possibility that the EV3 will miss when the degree value is *exactly* equal to zero and the motor will never stop. = | 0 is too specific of a case, so we program in < | 3 instead as a safety net; it will never fail, and will still get the turret into the center position.

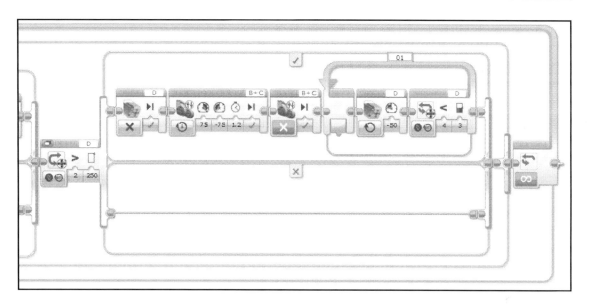

You can try experimenting with the target degree value to see how it affects the accuracy of the centering. If you set it to a smaller number (1 or 2 degrees), will the turret return to center more accurately, or does this make the turret rotate past center? Setting a larger target degree value (for example, 5 degrees) will make the turret stop just before reaching the center position. Give it a try!

Programming the left side

Now we need to tell the tank what to do if the turret has rotated too far to the left. The programming is going to be very similar to what we did for the right side. As a matter of fact, it is so similar that you may choose to copy the programming for the right side and make the changes from there. Since the left is the negative side, we need to change the sign on all degree and power values and flip the inequality signs.

Navigate to the *false* case of the most recent switch we added and add yet another switch. This one will be set up just like the last one: set the mode to **Motor Rotation** | **Compare** | **Degrees**, and the port to D. The only difference is we need to flip the inequality and negate the target value. So, change the compare type to < (type 4) and change the threshold value to −250 degrees:

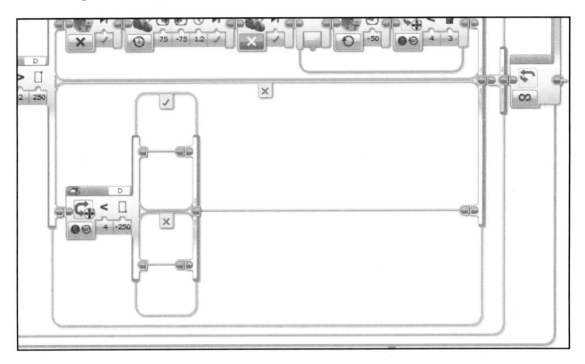

We will use the exact same blocks to program the return-to-center feature. Go through the code and negate all of the power and degree values, then change the inequality sign in the loop exit case from < (type 4) to > (type 2).

Negating all of the power and degree values and flipping the inequalities ensures that when the turret is too far left, it will execute the mirror image of the actions it would execute if the turret was too far to the right:

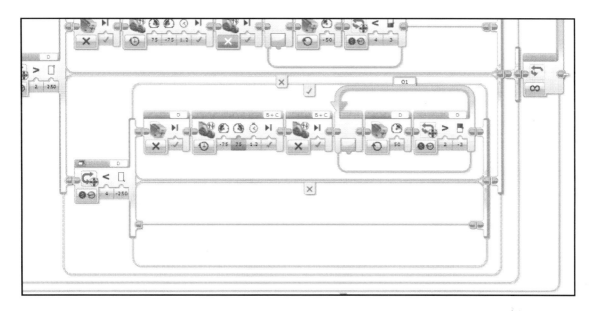

What do we put in the *false* case of this switch? Nothing again! That is because if the EV3 checks the turret position, and it is both not too far to the right and not too far to the left, it is within the acceptable range and we do not need to adjust it.

We have come to the end of our line of programming. When the EV3 gets to this point, it will loop back to the end and start the process all over again, allowing the tank to continuously follow the beacon.

Putting it all together

When you put all of the individual pieces together, the complete program will look like this:

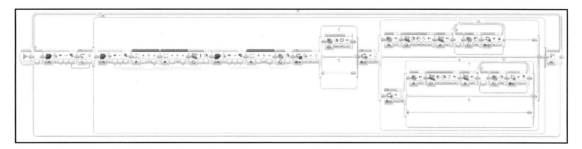

While the program may look large and confusing as a whole, remember that it becomes more manageable when you focus on individual parts of it. Check the program by tracing the path of the program flow through each block.

Congratulations! You have completed the program for the Security Tank! Now you can track beacons and keep your valuables safe from intruders.

Summary

We covered a lot in this chapter! Let's recap what we learned.

The focus of this project was to demonstrate how smart robots use infrared technology. Infrared is invisible to humans but can be detected by a robot's sensors, so it is a great option for when you want to invisibly control a robot. The tank robot uses two EV3 IR sensors to measure the position of an infrared beacon and follow it.

We also learned about some mechanical design concepts, that are applied to smart robots: tank treads and tank steering, turntables and cams, and using a motor to perform more than one function at a time. We briefly discussed gear ratios as they function in the tank; this is something we will explore further in the next chapter. We also discussed the importance of adding features that improve the visual impact of a smart robot.

We applied several different programming concepts such as using the heading and proximity values measured by an IR sensor in a program, loops and exit cases, using sensors to control logic (true/false) switches, proportional logic and k values, and programming a motor to return to center. We also programmed a safety case to keep a parameter within a desired range. In our Security Tank, we programmed some cases at the end that would make a large adjustment to the tank's path if necessary to keep the beacon in sight.

Finally, we learned about some decisions, or trade-offs, an engineer needs to consider when designing a smart robot. In the security tank, we saw a trade-off between ergonomics and making the robot smaller, as well as a trade-off between style and function. These are some of the common trade-offs you may encounter when you build you own smart robot.

In the next chapter, we will build the Omnilander, an all-terrain tank that can climb vertical obstacles. This project will apply tank tracks for a different purpose, and introduce proximity sensors and infrared remote control.

3
Omnilander – Ultimate All-Terrain Vehicle

Our second smart EV3 project is the Omnilander, a box-climbing robot. This is the ultimate all-terrain vehicle. Its large tank tracks give it traction over a diverse range of surfaces and allow it to drive up steep inclines. The Omnilander is also equipped with special hardware that allows it to climb up some vertical obstacles!

The Omnilander demonstrates some features that are used by smart robots in real life. For example, in this chapter, we will see how a smart robot can use advanced mechanisms such as worm gears, rack-and-pinion, and clutches to accomplish a goal using only one motor. We will review tank tracks and apply them for a slightly different purpose for this project. In this chapter, we will also introduce proximity sensors, which measure the distance between the sensor and an obstacle in a straight line. The Omnilander uses proximity sensors to avoid collisions and make decisions about whether it can climb an obstacle it encounters.

We will make two different programs for the Omnilander: the first is a **Remote Control (RC)** program, which will serve as an introduction to programming RC. The second program will be an autonomous program in which the Omnilander uses proximity sensors to drive around and climb obstacles without human intervention. We already used the EV3's infrared sensor for beacon tracking; in this chapter, we will take it two steps further and learn how to use it as an infrared receiver for RC and a proximity sensor for detecting obstacles. We will also use the EV3 IR beacon's functionality as a remote control.

Are you ready to build? Let's build the ultimate offroad machine:

Technical requirements

You must have EV3 Home Edition Software V1.2.2 or newer installed on your computer. You may also install LEGO Digital Designer (LDD) V4.3 and download the LDD file for this project to guide you in the building process.

The LDD file is available on the **Downloads** page of the the Builderdude35 website:

```
http://builderdude35.com/download/omnilander-ldd/
```

The LDD and EV3 files for this chapter are available on GitHub:

```
https://github.com/PacktPublishing/Building-Smart-LEGO-MINDSTORMS-EV3-Robots/
tree/master/Chapter03
```

Check out this video to see the robot in action:

```
https://goo.gl/PnrUKJ
```

Mechanical design

There are a lot of cool hardware features in this project. Let's discuss each one!

Drivetrain – tank tracks reapplied

Like the Security Tank we made in the last chapter, the Omnilander has two caterpillar tracks with tank-style steering. Recall that a robot with a tank drivetrain steers by varying the speed of the tracks on each side. In the Omnilander, one EV3 large motor powers each track; the left drive motor is plugged into port B and the right drive motor is plugged into port C.

The basic concept is the same for both robots, but the tracks themselves are different. While the Security Tank uses the rubber band-like tracks, the tracks on the Omnilander are made of the hard, grey plastic LEGO elements that clip together like a chain. Since the links are made of plastic, the tracks do not have sufficient traction on their own. The red rubber inserts are added to the tracks to increase traction. Flipping over the Omnilander gives us a clear view of the tracks:

Each of the Omnilander's tracks is guided by four sprockets. A sprocket is a gear-like wheel that drives a chain. The four sprockets are arranged so that the track links form a trapezoidal shape. The front of the track is steeply angled forward; this helps the Omnilander climb vertical obstacles, which we will discuss in more detail in the next section. The front top sprocket is the only one powered by the motor; the other three rotate freely to guide the track as it rotates:

The Omnilander's large treads are rugged and provide plenty of traction, enabling it to drive up steep slopes with ease. Now, we will add some hardware that will enable it to climb vertical obstacles.

Climbing mechanism

The Omnilander is equipped with special hardware that allows it to climb up some vertical obstacles, such as a small box. There are mechanisms in the front and back that lift the robot up and onto the obstacle:

The entire climbing mechanism is powered by one EV3 medium motor, plugged into port A. The motor routes its power through a long drive shaft that runs along the length of the robot:

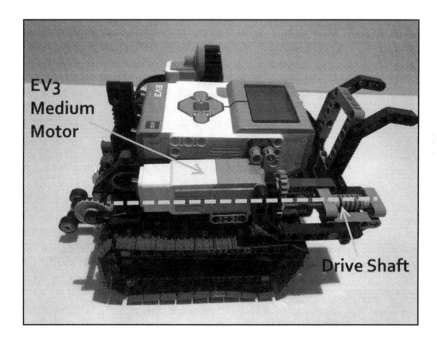

The drive shaft delivers the motor's power to the worm gear mechanism in the front of the robot and the jack in the rear.

Hook submechanism

On the front of the robot is a hook-like mechanism that grabs onto the box and pulls the robot up and onto the box. The mechanism is powered by a worm gear. A worm gear is a special spiral-shaped gear that works in conjunction with a traditional spur (circular) gear:

A few of the worm gear's special properties make it ideal for this application:

- A worm gear has a lot of mechanical reduction. Though the output is significantly slower than the input, the torque is multiplied; this is referred to as a mechanical advantage. The front hook mechanism needs to be strong enough to lift the Omnilander off the ground and pull it forward onto the box, and the worm gear provides a sufficient mechanical advantage to fulfill this requirement.

- A worm gear has a one-way rotation—the input can rotate the output, but the output cannot rotate the input. In the context of the Omnilander, this means that the motor can move the front hook, but no amount of force applied to the front hook can cause a rotation on the motor, which minimizes the mechanical stress on the motor.
- The worm gear mechanism redirects the motor's power 90 degrees. This makes for a streamlined mechanism because it eliminates the need for an additional 90-degree gear connection.

Because of the worm gear's one-way rotation, you cannot manually reset the climbing mechanism by pushing on the front hook (or any other part of the mechanism, for that matter). To manually reset the climbing mechanism, slide the 16-tooth gear connected to the medium motor's output so that it no longer meshes with the other 16-tooth gear beneath it. This will disengage the entire climbing mechanism from the motor. Then, you can move the climbing mechanism by rotating the worm gear directly by hand. In practice, this technique will look like this:

Ideally, the box that the Omnilander tries to climb should have a small lip on the edge to allow the hook to latch onto it. If there is no lip on the box, you may choose to add small rubber LEGO elements to the end of the hook to enable it to grip onto the box.

The worm gear is space-efficient and provides the hook with enough torque to lift the front of the Omnilander off the ground. But what lifts the rear of the robot?

Jack submechanism

The rear of the robot is lifted off the ground by a large rack-and-pinion mechanism that acts as a jack.

A rack gear is a long-toothed bar; think of it as a gear that has been unraveled with its teeth rolled out in a flat, straight line. The input of a rack-and-pinion system is a rotary (spinning) motion, which rotates the circular pinion gear. The pinion gear interfaces with the rack gear and causes the rack gear to slide in a straight line; the motor's torque has been converted to a linear motion. This linear motion lifts up the rear of the Omnilander. When the motor turns, the rack extends downward and pushes the rear of the robot off the ground.

 Any mechanical system that takes rotary motion as an input and converts it to linear motion is called a linear actuator. Therefore, this rack-and-pinion system is a linear actuator; the system converts the motor's rotational torque into a straight-line motion.

At the bottom end of the rack is a sled with two small wheels; when the Omnilander lifts itself off the ground, the sled allows the robot to slide forward as the front hook pulls it forward towards the box:

Although the rack-and-pinion mechanism is the staple of the jack system, there are a few other important components that allow the system to work smoothly. Before the motor's torque reaches the rack-and-pinion, it is redirected through a 90-degree gear connection, which has some mechanical reduction. The torque is then sent through a second set of gears, which reduces the rotation further. The total gear ratio before reaching the rack-and-pinion is 5:1. That means the motor must spin five full times to rotate the pinion gear once.

Although that may seem like a lot of reduction, it is still quite a bit less than the reduction provided by the worm gear on the front of the robot. This means that the rack gear reaches its mechanical limit sooner than the worm gear. This is a problem, because the entire climbing mechanism is connected by one drive shaft; when the rack gear reaches its mechanical limit, it will seize up the entire mechanism and prevent the robot from completing its climb. To solve this issue, one of the aforementioned gears in the rear-jack mechanism is replaced with a clutch gear; note the large, white gear in the gear train at the back of the robot.

The clutch gear introduces just the right amount of slip into the system: it grips and transfers power to the rack until it reaches its mechanical limit. At that point, the clutch gear begins to slip, which allows the front hook to keep moving while keeping the jack stationary. The clutch gear prevents the entire mechanism from locking up.

When the front hook and rear jack work together, the result is a smooth, cohesive climbing action. The climbing mechanism as a whole is fairly complex with a lot of moving parts. However, the complexity pays off because the mechanism automatically coordinates all of the motions necessary for a successful climb. Therefore, we can consider the hardware to be smart!

Proximity sensors

The Omnilander is equipped with two sensors. The ultrasonic sensor (also known as the US sensor) is plugged into port 1 and is located low in the front of the robot between the two tracks. The infrared sensor (also known as the IR sensor) is located on the left side of the robot, closer to the back of the robot than the US sensor:

The left and right sides refer to the perspective of a person standing behind the robot, looking at the back. This way of identifying the left and right sides is standard for robots and cars. When working on a project with a teammate, always make sure that you are referring to the correct side.

Ultrasonic sensor

The EV3's **Ultrasonic (US)** sensor is a proximity sensor, meaning that it measures the distance between itself and an object. An ultrasonic sensor measures distance by emitting a high-frequency sound that humans cannot hear. The US sensor then waits for the sound to bounce off of the object and return to the sensor. Using the time it took for the sound to travel away from and return to the sensor, the EV3 can estimate the distance between the sensor and the obstacle. This makes for an accurate sensor that is not susceptible to light interference. However, the surface of the object needs to be perpendicular to the sensor, otherwise the sound may not return to the sensor and the distance cannot be estimated. The US sensor is used in the Omnilander's autonomous program:

Infrared sensor

We introduced the IR sensor in the last chapter, where we discussed its ability to measure the position of an infrared beacon. The Omnilander will use the IR sensor's two other functions. In addition to tracking a beacon, the IR sensor can act as a proximity sensor to measure distance (similar to the US sensor), and it can read the commands sent by the EV3 remote control. The Omnilander uses proximity sensor mode in its autonomous program and receiver mode for the RC program.

Programming

Now, we will write some code that will bring our smart robot to life. We will make two programs; the first is an RC program, and the second is an autonomous exploration program.

RC

This program allows the user to control the Omnilander using the EV3 infrared remote. The infrared sensor receives the commands sent by the remote. The robot is programmed to respond to each of the remote commands. Using the remote, the user can drive the Omnilander around and deploy the climbing mechanism to scale a vertical obstacle:

Although the user controls the robot, some of the robot's processes are still automated, so this can still be considered a *smart* program.

This is a simple tank-control RC program, which can be adapted and used with any tank-style robot. Later in this book, we will revisit RC when we make a more sophisticated program for the Falcon race car.

Setting up the loop

All of the code for the Omnilander is contained within an infinite loop, which makes the program repeat until the user presses the back button on the EV3 brick to exit the program and return to the menu. Recall that we did the same thing with the Security Tank; most of the programs we will make in this book will be contained within an infinite loop:

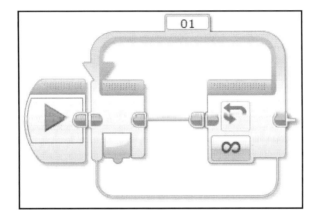

When you add the loop block into the program, it will be set to repeat infinitely by default. This is exactly what we want, so there is no need to change any of the settings. We are ready to move on!

Setting up the switch

When a button is pressed on the remote control, it sends a command. The infrared sensor attached to the EV3 brick will receive this command and, using this information, the EV3 brick can determine which button or combination of buttons was pressed.

At the heart of the RC program is a switch. The switch uses the IR sensor to read the signals sent by the infrared remote. Then, the switch chooses to execute one of its cases depending on the combination of buttons that was pressed on the remote.

Add a switch block into your program. Make sure that it is placed within the loop. Then, change the mode of the switch to **Infrared Sensor** | **Measure** | **Remote**. This puts the IR sensor into receiver mode. The IR sensor on the Omnilander is in port 4, so the default port setting on the switch is correct. Remember to match the channel on the remote to the channel specified on the switch:

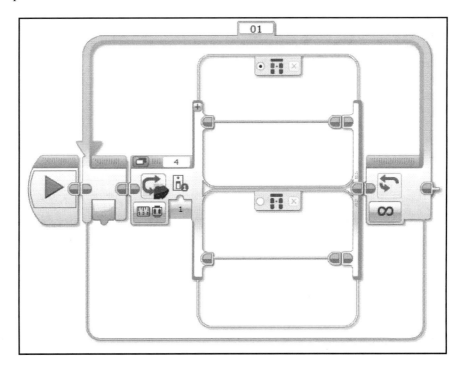

By default, the switch has two cases. With the switch set to **Infrared Sensor** | **Measure** | **Remote**, we have the option to add more cases to the switch, which allows the robot to respond to more button commands. We will need more cases for this specific RC program, so press the **Add Case** button eight times for a total of 10 switch cases:

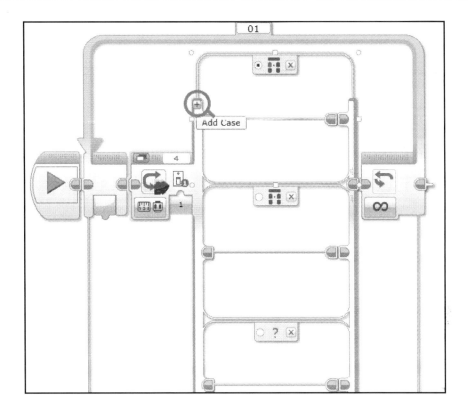

Configuring the switch cases

We have a switch with the correct number of cases, but we need to set up each case. For each case, we will do two things: first, we need to define the combination of buttons that will activate that case, then we will need to write the code that we want the EV3 to execute when that case is active.

Though this RC program is fairly straightforward, this is where the program can become monotonous and confusing. We have 10 cases to program, so writing this program will get pretty repetitive. Not to worry though, because soon you will have a working RC program!

The first case to set up is our default *nothing* case. This case will execute when none of the remote buttons are pressed and it will stop all of the robot's motors. To define the button combination, click on the tab at the top of the switch case and select button ID **0**, no buttons pressed. Because this is the default case (when nothing happens, the robot stops), click the circle on the left side of that tab to assign this case as the *default case*; this is something that we will only do for this case. Finally, program what you want the robot to do when no remote buttons are pressed: add a move tank block into the case and simply set its mode to **Off**. Your completed first case should look like this:

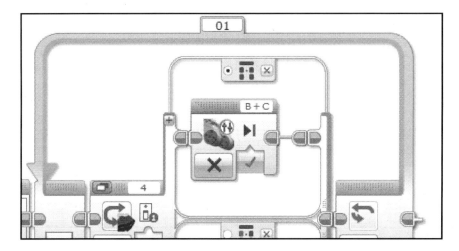

Then, we move on to our second case. This one will execute when only the top-left button is pressed, and it will cause the Omnilander's left track to drive forward, resulting in a right turn. Define the button combination using the tab at the top of this new case; we will need button ID **1** here. Then, program the action that the robot will complete: add a move tank block and set its mode to **On**. Set the power for each drive motor: enter a power value of −100 for the left motor (port B) and a power value of 0 for the right motor (port C). This will spin the left track forward at full power while the right track is stopped.

Why do we need to set a negative power for the Omnilander to drive forward? This has to do with the drive motor's orientation within the robot chassis. In this specific robot, the drive motors are upside down relative to their normal position, so the direction that the motor spins is mirrored. If you recall when we programmed the Security Tank, we did not have to negate the motor powers because the drive motors were in the more conventional *normal* orientation.

For future reference, when programming the Omnilander's drive motors, remember that a negative power will make the robot drive forward, and that positive power will make it drive in reverse.

The completed second case should look like this:

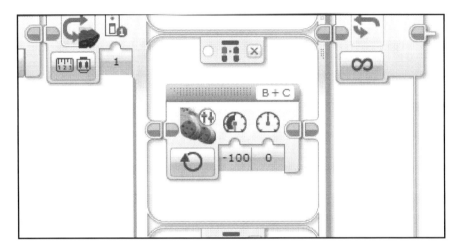

Now, we are ready for our third case. This one will execute when only the bottom-left button is pressed and cause the left track to drive in reverse, resulting in a reverse left turn. Define the button combination (ID **2**) and add a move tank block. Set the block's mode to **On**, and set the power of the left drive motor to 100, and the power of the right side to 0:

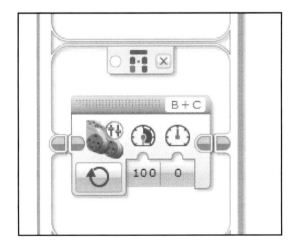

Case four runs when only the top-right remote button is pressed and drives the right track forward, causing the Omnilander to make a left turn. Select button ID **3** and add a move tank block. Set its mode to **On** and set the power values to 0 (left) and -100 (right):

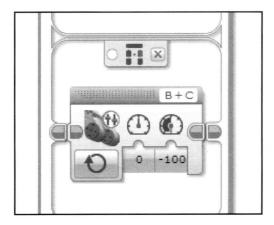

Case five runs when only the bottom-right button is pressed. This case drives the right track in reverse, which makes the robot do a right turn in reverse. Select button ID **4** and set up the move tank block with a left motor power value of 0 and a right power value of 100:

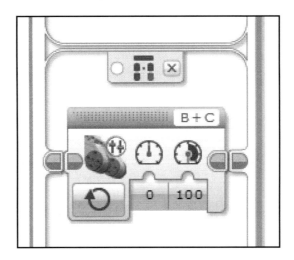

See how this type of programming can get repetitive and monotonous after a while? That is because we need to tell the robot what to do for each possible combination of buttons that we plan to use. At this point, we are halfway finished.

Now, we need to program the instructions for when two buttons are pressed simultaneously. With tank-style steering, each track is controlled independently, so this is how you get the robot to drive forward, reverse, or make a spin turn.

Our first two-button case executes when both top buttons are pressed. This will drive both the left and right tracks forward to make the tank drive forward in a straight line. Select button ID **5** and set up a move tank block with both drive motors set to a power of -100:

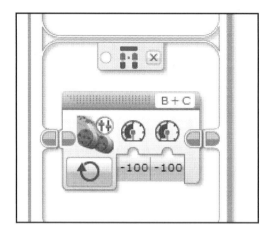

What if the left-front button is pressed at the same time as the bottom-right button? The robot will drive its left tread forward while spinning its right tread in reverse. This will cause it to do a clockwise spin turn. Select the button combination (ID **6**) and add a move tank block; set the left drive motor power to -100 and the right motor power to 100:

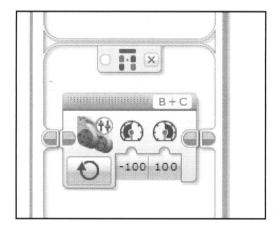

Now, we will program the mirror image: if the bottom-left button and the top-right button are pressed simultaneously, the robot will do a counter-clockwise spin turn. Select button ID 7 and set up the move tank block accordingly; the power values will also be a mirror image, with the left motor power set to 100 and the right motor power set to -100:

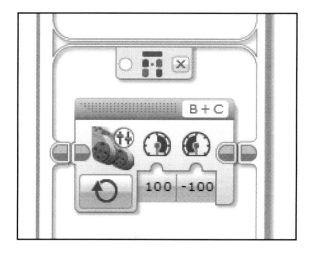

If both bottom buttons are pressed, the Omnilander will drive in a straight line in reverse. Select button ID 8 and program in a move tank block with both drive motors set to a power level of 100:

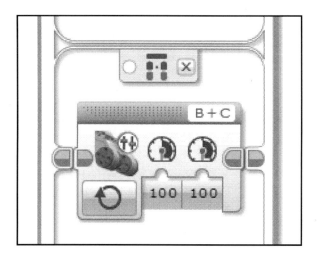

The final case executes when the large toggle button at the top of the remote is pressed. This will trigger the automated climbing sequence to get the Omnilander to climb over an obstacle. The button ID for this case is **9**.

This case will have three motor blocks. The first is a medium motor block, which deploys the climbing mechanism and hoists the Omnilander over the obstacle. Set the medium motor block to **On for Rotations** and make sure motor port A is selected. Then, set the motor to spin at -100 power for 14 full rotations.

The second block in the sequence is a move tank block. This block drives the robot onto the obstacle after it has lifted itself up. This block should be set to **On for Seconds**, with both drive motors turning at -35 percent power for 1.4 seconds.

The final block is another medium motor block. This block simply retracts the climbing mechanism to allow the Omnilander to drive away. So, this block will be the same as the first (**On for Rotations**, 14 rotations), with the only difference being that the power is set to 100 to get the motor to turn in the opposite direction:

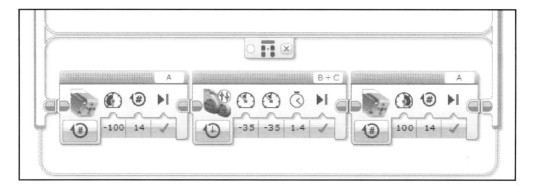

Why is the programming for the climbing sequence so simple? It is because in this robot, the difficult work is done by the hardware. The programming can be as simple as turning motor A on for 14 rotations because more effort was put into designing a sophisticated mechanical system that could coordinate many of the actions by itself. Therefore, you can say that the hardware in this robot is pretty smart! Compare this to the Security Tank, which had simpler hardware but more complex software. This is another decision you may need to consider when making your own smart robot: whether to make the hardware more sophisticated to simplify the software, or vice versa. You will make this decision based on your available materials, the goal you are trying to accomplish, and your own skills.

That is the completed RC program! Although it took a while to make, you can now control the Omnilander with the remote control and explore its off-roading capabilities.

Autonomous mode

This program allows the Omnilander to operate without human intervention. The robot will drive around autonomously and use its proximity sensors to avoid collisions. It will also use its proximity sensors to estimate the height of a vertical obstacle and determine whether it can climb over it. If it decides that the obstacle is low enough, the Omnilander will run its automated climbing procedure to scale the obstacle.

Setting up the loop and switches

As with the RC program, the first step is to add an infinite loop into which the rest of the code will be placed:

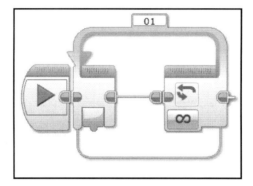

The EV3 will first check the status of the US sensor (port 1). Since this sensor is mounted low, it will see almost all of the obstacles that the Omnilander will encounter. If the US sensor sees an obstacle that is less than 20 centimeters away, the robot knows that a collision is imminent and it must decide whether to climb or steer away.

To program this step, add a switch block and set its mode to **Ultrasonic Sensor** | **Compare** | **Distance Centimeters**. Make sure that you select sensor port 1. Then, set the threshold value; the EV3 should be looking for a distance value of less than 20 centimeters (< | 20):

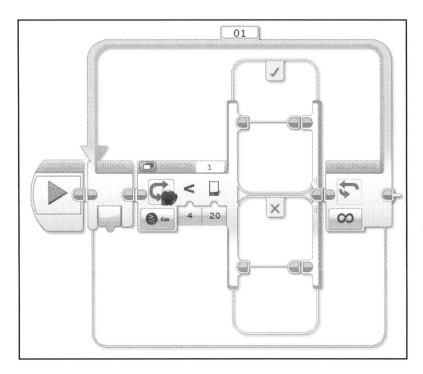

Programming the false case

We will program the false case for this switch first because it is very straightforward. This case executes when the US sensor does not see an obstacle within 20 centimeters of its current position. There are no nearby obstacles, so the Omnilander does not need to take any action to avoid a collision. Therefore, the robot can simply continue driving forward.

In the false case of the US sensor switch, simply place a move tank block. Set its mode to **On** and set the power level to −75 for both drive motors. This will keep the robot driving in a straight line until the US sensor sees a nearby obstacle:

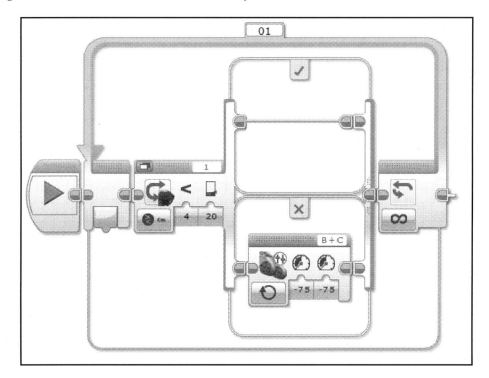

Programming the true case

What happens if the US sensor does detect an obstacle within 20 centimeters? This means that a collision is imminent and the EV3 must make a decision: attempt to climb over the obstacle or steer to avoid it.

The autonomous program decides which action to take based off of the reading on the IR sensor, which is in the high position. If the IR sensor also detects the obstacle, the robot knows the obstacle is too high to climb, and it must steer to avoid it. However, if the upper sensor does not see the obstacle, the robot knows that the obstacle is low enough and it will attempt to climb it:

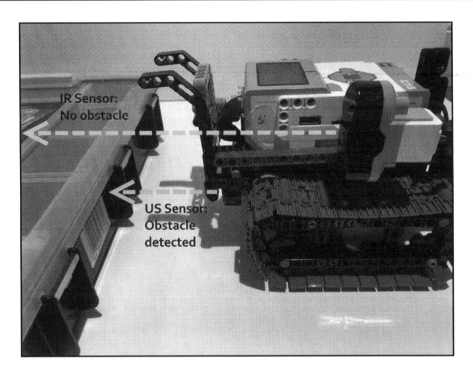

We program this decision using another switch, this time using the IR sensor in port 4. The switch's mode should be set to **Infrared Sensor | Compare | Proximity**. As you can likely guess, this makes use of the IR sensor's proximity functionality (the Security Tank used the beacon tracking function, and the RC program we just made uses its functionality as an infrared receiver).

Verify that port 4 is selected. Then, set the threshold value to less than 35 centimeters (< | 35). This value is slightly larger than the US sensor's threshold value of 20 centimeters because the IR sensor is mounted farther back on the robot than the US sensor.

When you finish setting up your IR sensor switch, it will look like this:

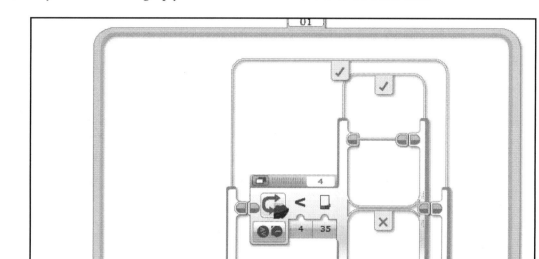

Programming the obstacle avoidance sequence

If both proximity sensors see the obstacle, the obstacle is too tall to climb and the Omnilander will steer to avoid it and continue on in a new direction.

Add two move tank blocks to the *true* case of the IR sensor switch. Change the mode of the first block to **On for Seconds**. Then, set the power levels of each of the drive motors: the left motor should be set to a power of 0 percent, and the right motor should be set to 100 percent. Set the duration of the turn to 1.8 seconds. This makes the robot perform an approximately 90-degree right turn in reverse. Finally, change the mode of the second move tank block to **Off**. This will momentarily clear the power values assigned to each drive motor:

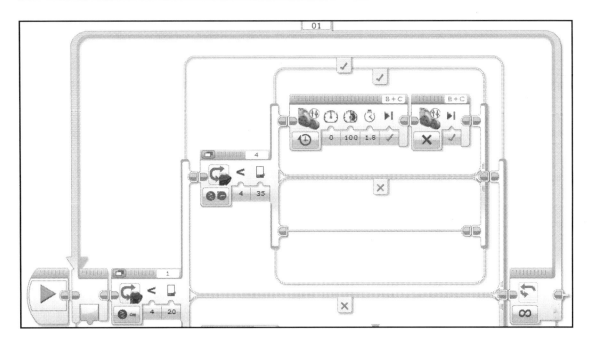

At this point, if the proximity sensors no longer see an obstacle when the turn is complete, the obstacle has been avoided successfully and the Omnilander will continue driving in this new direction. If the path is still not clear, the robot will repeat the turn until the proximity sensors no longer detect an obstacle.

The 90-degree turn is simple but not necessarily the most elegant solution. You may choose to change the style of turn to make obstacle avoidance smoother. You can even try adding additional sensors to make a more sophisticated obstacle avoidance sequence.

Programming the climbing sequence

If the IR sensor does not see the obstacle, then the obstacle is low enough that the Omnilander can attempt to climb it. The climbing sequence will be programmed into the *false* case of the IR sensor switch.

The climbing sequence will be similar to the one we made for the RC program. The first block is a move tank block set to **On for Seconds**, and it will power both drive motors forward at -35 percent power for 1.8 seconds. This block allows the robot to close the 20-centimeter gap between it and the obstacle it just detected.

Now, the robot is in position to climb the obstacle. The remainder of the climbing sequence is identical to the one we made for the RC program. A medium motor block rotates the motor in port A for 14 rotations at -100 percent power to deploy the climbing mechanism and pull the Omnilander up and onto the obstacle. The move tank block drives the tracks forward at -35 percent power for 1.4 seconds to move the robot completely onto the obstacle. Finally, the last medium motor block runs the motor in port A at 100 percent power for 14 rotations to retract the climbing equipment:

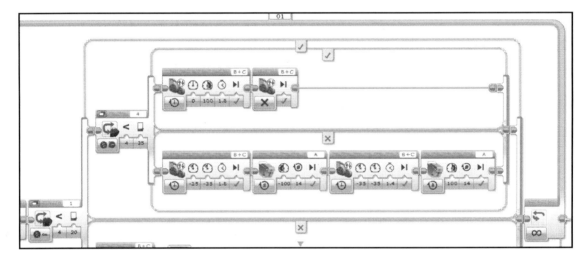

After that, the program repeats; the EV3 reads its sensors again to determine which of the conditions to run.

Putting it all together

When all of the pieces are put into place, the complete autonomous program looks like this:

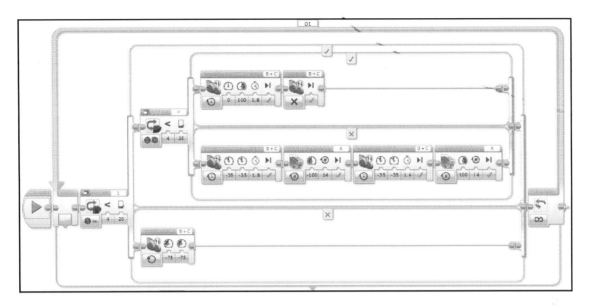

Now you have completed two programs for the Omnilander! You are ready to traverse some extreme terrain!

Summary

That was a lot of information, so let's summarize the key ideas.

For the first time, we saw how well-designed hardware can coordinate a complex action on its own and decrease the complexity of the software; we can consider this hardware to be smart. We also expanded our knowledge of mechanisms. We revisited tank treads and used a sturdier construction with more traction that was more suitable for the Omnilander's off-road application. We learned about how worm gears are a convenient way to obtain a mechanical advantage and one-way rotation within a compact footprint. We created our first application for the rack-and-pinion mechanism, a type of linear actuator; we will use rack-and-pinion for a different application later in this book when we build the Falcon race car. Lastly, we saw how a clutch gear can introduce some slip to prevent a gear train from jamming up.

We used the IR sensor again, but this time we used two different functionalities of the sensor: we used the sensor as a receiver for a remote control and as a proximity sensor. We also introduced the US sensor, a very accurate type of proximity sensor.

We reviewed some of the programming techniques we learned in the last chapter and built on our knowledge with some new techniques. We programmed a pair of proximity sensors and used them together in the program to help the robot make some decisions about how to react to its environment. We programmed an infrared receiver and made our first tank-style RC program, which we will expand upon when we make the Falcon race car. We revisited feedback loops and reapplied our knowledge of switches to use them for new sensors.

Finally, we learned about another important decision that you may need to make when you make your own smart robot: whether to make the hardware more complex to simplify the software, or vice versa. This is a decision you will make based on your engineering goals, your available materials, and your own personal skill set.

In the next chapter, we will be looking at the engineering at work behind one of the original EV3 one-kit wonders, the famous Timmyton!

4
Timmyton – Interactive Robotic Shark

Next, we will be building the Timmyton, an interactive robotic shark that features a myriad of cool functions and has a unique personality. This robot has become a popular MINDSTORMS icon because it can be built using only the parts from one EV3 retail set (31313), making it accessible to young robotics enthusiasts. It was among the first robots to feature a custom GUI, which streamlines five different operating modes within one program.

In this chapter, we will take a look at how the Timmyton manages to have so many mechanical features and such a compact footprint. We will examine each of the simple machines that work together to animate the Timmyton.

The Timmyton's sophisticated programming makes it a great example of a smart robot. We will program the Timmyton's custom GUI, which will give you the knowledge you need to make a GUI for your own smart robot. GUI's have other applications within the world of LEGO robotics, including FIRST LEGO League. Then, we will program the Timmyton's operating modes. We will revisit some previously learned concepts, such as beacon tracking, remote control, and tank steering, but also introduce some new concepts, such as the color sensor. Perhaps most importantly, we will discuss how different elements of the programming contribute to the Timmyton's unique personality.

What are we waiting for? It is time to make this iconic EV3 smart robot:

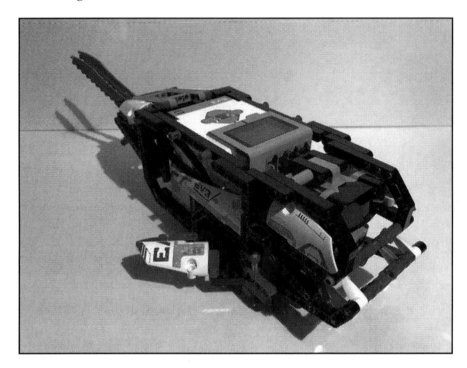

Technical requirements

You must have EV3 Home Edition Software V1.2.2 or newer installed on your computer. You may also install LEGO Digital Designer (LDD) V4.3 and download the LDD file for this project to guide you in the building process.

The LDD file is available on the **Downloads** page of the the Builderdude35 website:

http://builderdude35.com/download/timmyton-ldd/

The LDD and EV3 files for this chapter are available on GitHub:

https://github.com/PacktPublishing/Building-Smart-LEGO-MINDSTORMS-EV3-Robots/tree/master/Chapter04

Check out this video to see the robot in action:

https://goo.gl/zfLcf8

Mechanical design

We will start by dissecting the physical components that make this one-kit wonder tick.

Drivetrain

Like the Omnilander and the Security Tank, the Timmyton uses tank-style steering to drive around. However, one glaringly obvious difference should jump out at you—the Timmyton does not have tank tracks! How can it have tank-style steering without having tank tracks?

Even though there are no tank tracks, the drivetrain is still classified as tank-style because the Timmyton steers by varying the power sent to each side. In place of tank tracks, the Timmyton has wheels. One wheel is directly connected to each EV3 large drive motor. The ports for the drive motors follow the typical EV3 convention: the left drive motor is plugged into port B, and the right drive motor is in port C. The two drive wheels are tucked tightly together within the chassis so that they do not disrupt the Timmyton's shark-like appearance:

The robot needs a third point on which it can distribute its weight. Near the rear of the robot is a caster wheel. A caster wheel is a small wheel mounted on a vertical axle so that it can swivel in any direction. A caster wheel was chosen for the Timmyton because it can pivot in any direction, meaning it will follow the front two wheels wherever they steer, ensuring maneuverability in every direction. Caster wheels are the go-to choice whenever an engineer needs a floating wheel that will support the machine's weight without hindering mobility:

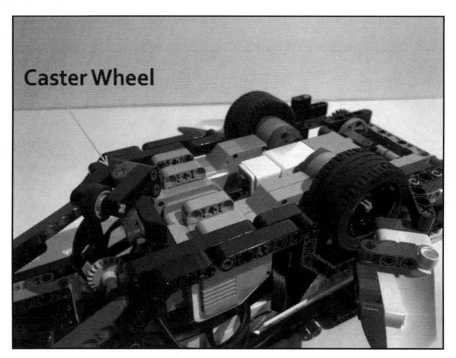

Cosmetics

When designing the Timmyton, considerable effort was put into designing its exterior. Visual impact is imperative for the Timmyton, more so than either of the other robots we have made so far. If you are building a shark-like robot, you need to make sure that it looks the part! Several aspects of the Timmyton were designed with a purely cosmetic purpose so that the robot is instantly recognizable as a shark.

Chassis

The Timmyton's chassis was carefully designed to have a fish-like silhouette. At the center is a rectangular frame that houses the EV3 brick and all three of the motors. A snout-like sub-frame protrudes from the front of the core chassis. In the back, a triangle-shaped frame tapers the chassis down into the tail to complete the sleek, hydrodynamic profile:

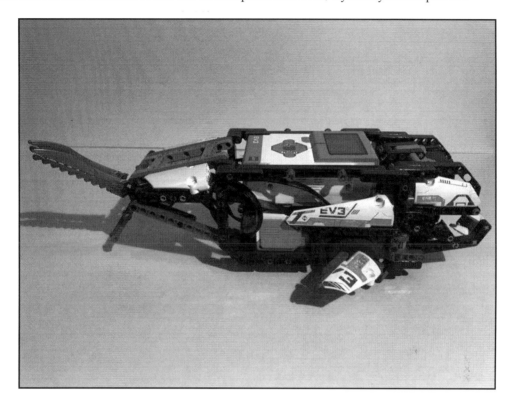

Pectoral fins

What would a shark be without its fins? On either side of the chassis, a fin protrudes from the Timmyton's profile. The fins are made from the short, curved EV3 panels placed on an angle beam. The fins' secondary purpose is to hide the drive wheels:

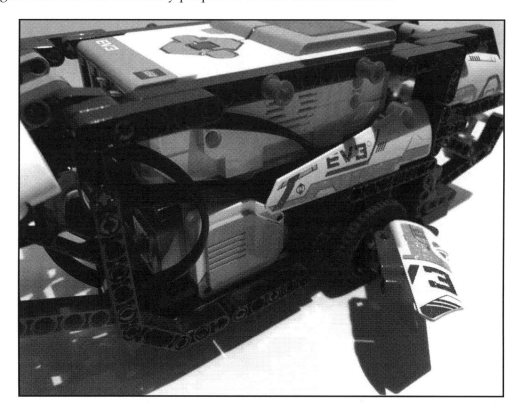

Jaws

One of the first things that come to mind when you hear the word *shark* is a pair of powerful jaws filled with sharp teeth. Thankfully, the Timmyton has this covered! Its huge jaw opens wide, ready to chomp on some LEGO bricks. The white tooth-like elements included in the EV3 set serve as the Timmyton's teeth:

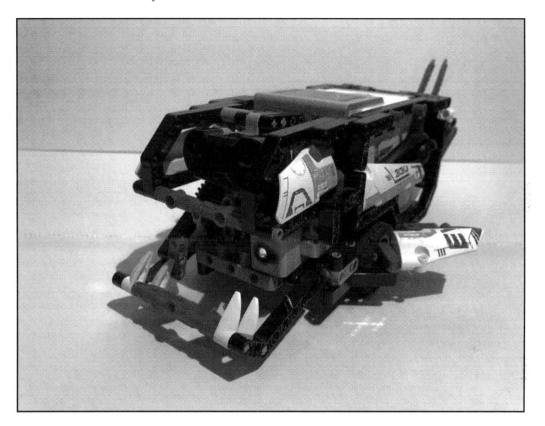

Tail

A slender tail made of the long red blade elements included in the EV3 set completes the visual package:

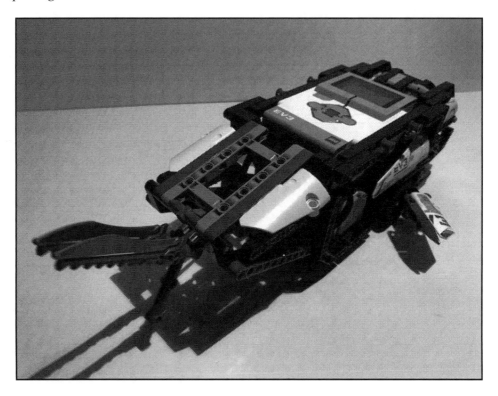

Now that the decorative jaws and tail are in place, we need to get them to move! That will add an extra dimension to the Timmyton's visual impact, make it more interactive, and enhance the overall wow factor.

Animating the jaws and tail

The Timmyton's jaws and tail are motorized by the same EV3 medium motor, which is plugged into port A. The medium motor is situated between the two drive motors.

A special gearbox splits the medium motor's power so it can simultaneously power the jaws in the front and the tail in the rear. A bevel gear directly attached to the medium motor's output meshes with two gear trains; it meshes with another bevel gear through a 90-degree connection to transfer power to the jaws, as well as a set of gears located above it, which transfer power to the tail.

Bevel gears are a special type of gear; they have a conventional circular shape like spur gears, but the corners of their teeth are cut at an angle. This allows them to form 90-degree connections with one another while still being able to form conventional parallel gear meshes like spur gears can. The Timmyton takes advantage of the bevel gear's ability to form both types of connections; this is how the Timmyton splits the power from one motor within a compact footprint.

The gearbox is visible on the underside of the robot near the mouth:

Chomping jaws

The 90-degree bevel gear connection increases the motor's rotation speed by a ratio of 1:1.67, increasing the speed of the jaw. A pair of 24-tooth spur gears transfers the power higher. A five-stud beam links the lower jaw to the top spur gear. The beam is connected off-center on the gear, giving the gear a cam-like effect, causing the beam to reciprocate. As a result, the jaws continuously cycle up and down when the medium motor spins:

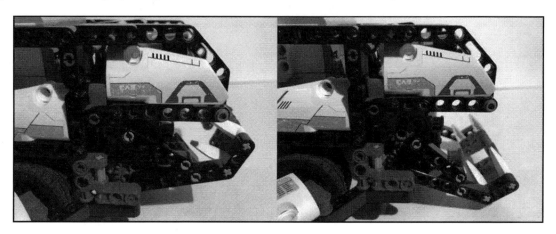

Wagging tail

A long driveshaft that runs nearly the entire length of the robot transfers the motor's power rearward to animate the tail. The motor's power is redirected through a 90-degree connection and slightly reduced by a ratio of 1.67:1. This is coincidentally the inverse of the gear ratio used to transfer power to the jaws, which means that the tail cycles slower than the mouth.

After the power is redirected to 90 degrees, a cam mechanism produces a reciprocating motion through the connected rod. The rod connects to the tail, causing it to continuously cycle left and right as the motor spins. Sounds familiar, right? This is similar to the cam mechanism used to cycle the jaws.

The cam mechanism that animates the tail is located at the rear of the robot:

The best part about using cams to move the jaws and tail is that both will cycle continuously as the motor spins. So, all you have to do is set the motor to run continuously at a desired speed and the mechanisms do the rest!

Sensors

The Timmyton incorporates two sensors into its design—an infrared sensor and a color sensor. The program makes full use of each of these sensors' functions to create a rich interactive experience.

Infrared sensor

An EV3 infrared sensor (port 4) is located in the Timmyton's nose, giving it a clear line of sight to any obstacle or an infrared remote. We have already used the IR sensor extensively, so this will all be a review. The Timmyton's program makes use of all three of the IR sensor's functions: proximity sensor, receiver, and beacon tracker:

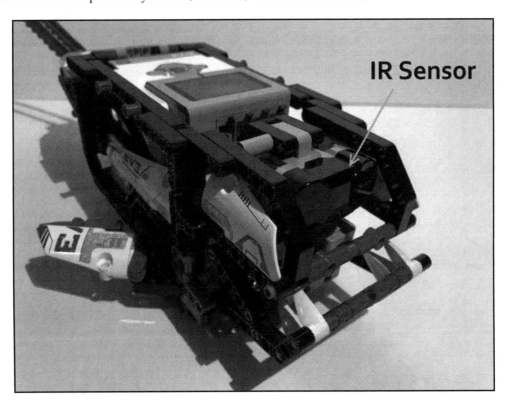

Color sensor

The color sensor, plugged into port 3, is located in the Timmyton's mouth. The color sensor is used in **Hungry** mode, when the sensor gives the robot a sense of taste. You can feed the Timmyton LEGO bricks, and it will react differently to each *flavor* block you feed it. When a LEGO brick is placed in the Timmyton's mouth, the color sensor will recognize the color of the brick. Each color represents a different flavor, and the Timmyton will react differently to each one.

In the next section, we will program **Hungry** mode, among other interactive features:

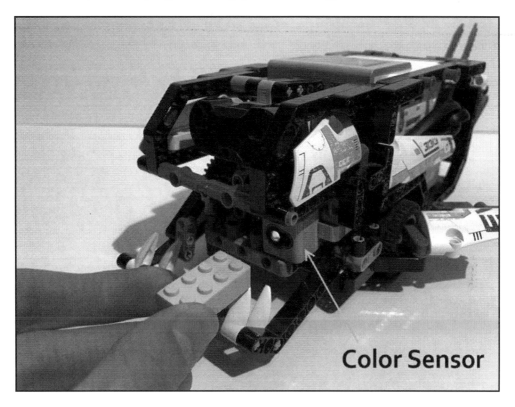

Color Sensor

Programming

The Timmyton's program is very complex, more so than anything we have made so far. That is because it is essentially five programs rolled into one, plus the programming for the GUI. Don't fret, though! There will be plenty of new concepts, but at the same time, a good chunk of the programming will be reviewed from the previous few chapters. We will walk through this step by step in a neat, orderly fashion.

Now, it is time to program some interactive features and bring the Timmyton to life.

GUI

When the user starts the Timmyton's program, he or she will be greeted by this screen on the EV3 display:

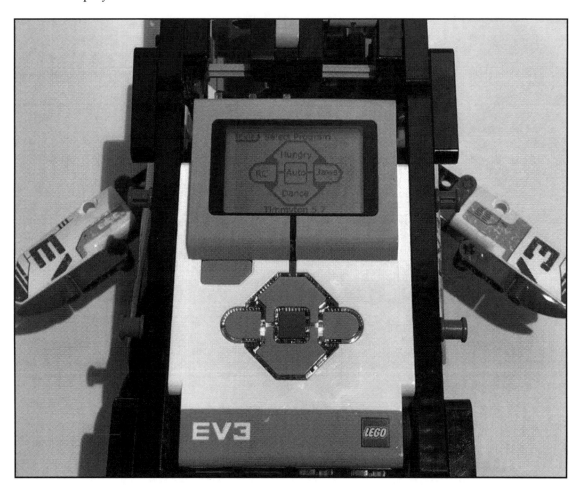

This is the Timmyton's graphical user interface, or GUI, which allows the user to select one of five operating modes within the same program. After selecting an operating mode, the user can exit and return to this menu screen to select a new operating mode. Pressing the back button on the EV3 brick at any time will exit the whole program and return the EV3 back to its home screen.

The Timmyton's custom GUI is among the robot's most innovative features. It streamlines all of the robot's programs into one user-friendly package. This added ease of use enhances the Timmyton's fun factor and has helped contribute to its popularity.

A GUI has additional applications within the realm of LEGO robotics—many **FIRST LEGO League** (FLL) teams have decided to use custom GUI's and/or program sequencers to make changing programs quicker and easier, saving precious time on the competition field. In the real world, a GUI is used to ease interaction between people and machines. The Windows operating system is a real-world example of a GUI; it makes using a computer easier and more accessible by presenting the computer's features, functions, and programs in a way that is easier for people who are not computer experts to understand.

Now, let's program the GUI! Keep in mind that while we are making this one for the Timmyton, you can follow these same steps to make a different one for your own smart robot.

Creating the menu graphics

We will use the EV3 programming environment's built-in **Image Editor** to make the menu graphics. In the top-left corner, click on **Tools** | **Image Editor** to pull it up. In the **Image Editor**, you can draw, write text, import and modify images, and save them to use them in your program.

The home screen for the Timmyton was created by importing an image of the EV3 brick buttons, cleaning it up a bit, then typing the names of the corresponding operating modes onto each button:

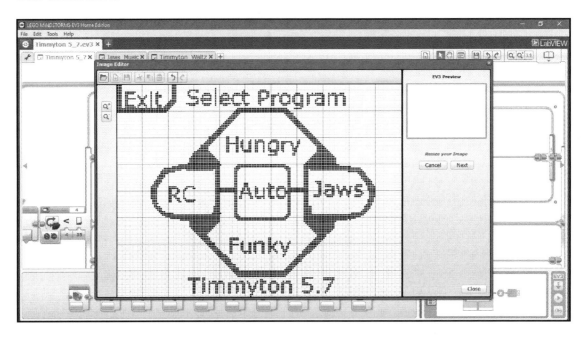

The number **5.7** after the Timmyton's name on the menu graphic indicates that the current version of the Timmyton is 5.7. It took many revisions to refine the Timmyton to the polished state it is in now. As a matter of fact, all of the robots featured in this book have been revised at least once from their original designs. Keep this in mind when you build your own smart robot. It is very rare that an engineer gets a project perfect on the first try, so do not be afraid to experiment and continue modifying your design!

You will also need to make a graphic for each of the operating modes so the user knows which one is active. There is no need for anything fancy here; you can simply type the name of the operating mode on the screen. Here is the display for Funky mode for reference:

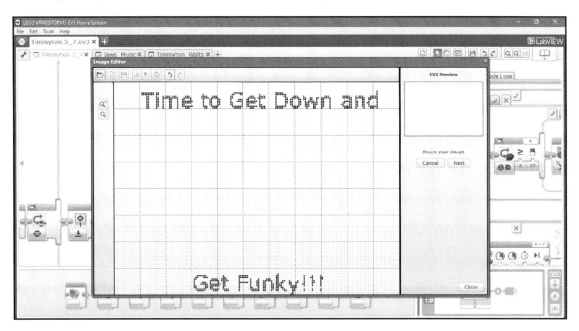

Programming the GUI

We will start the program the same way we have started every program so far: with an infinite loop that encloses the rest of the program.

Then, add in some code to start making the GUI. These first few blocks are for initialization. The blocks, in order, do the following—clear the EV3 display, print the custom menu to the display, stop all of the motors, then set the brick LED to blink green. The Timmyton makes extensive use of the brick LED to add an extra dimension to the user-robot interaction:

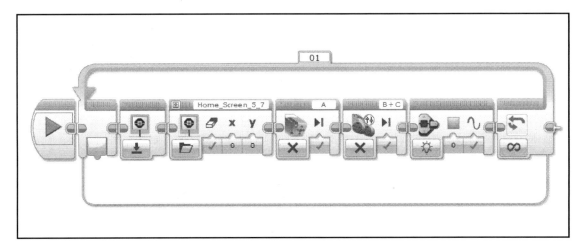

After the initialization code, insert a switch block. Change its mode to **Brick Buttons** | **Measure** | **Brick Buttons**. Make sure that you activate tabbed view; otherwise, the program will become too cumbersome and confusing.

This switch is very important because all of the programming for the operating modes will go inside. Each mode is a case within the switch, and when a brick button is pressed, the switch will activate the corresponding operating mode:

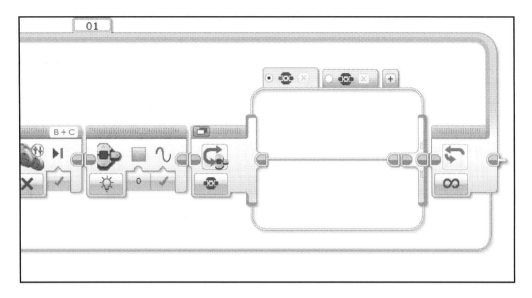

Next, set up the cases. There are two by default, so add four more for a total of six. Assign each brick button to its own case. Finally, set the blank case (not buttons pressed) as the default case:

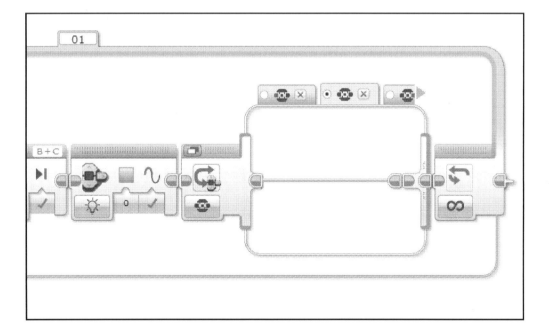

Each case needs to have some of the same basic programming within it—a display reset block, a block to print the name of the operating mode to the display, and finally a loop block.

The loop block must be named `Mode Loop`. You can name a loop by clicking on the tab at the top and typing the name in. This is the first time that we have needed to name a loop; it is imperative that we do this because we will refer to this loop from another part of the code when we program the loop interrupt:

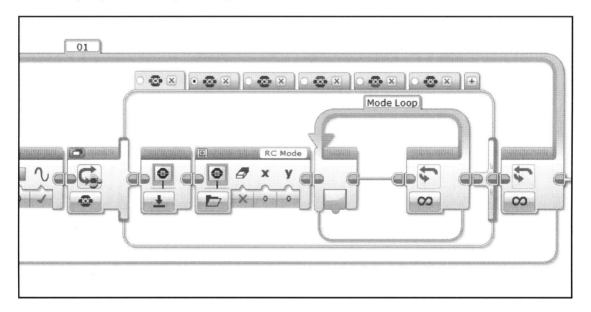

Now, time for something totally new: dragging out another start block! Place it beneath the line of code blocks we were just working on. We are making a second task, a small piece of code that will run simultaneously in parallel with the main task. Add an infinite loop to this new branch. Within the loop, add a wait block, set its mode to **Brick Buttons** | **Compare** | **Brick Buttons**, select the center brick button as the one to monitor (button ID **2**), and set the state to 2. The wait is set up so that the program will proceed when the center brick button is pressed and released. Finally, add a loop interrupt block directly after the wait. Select `Mode Loop`, the loop we just set up, by clicking the top-right corner of the loop interrupt block.

This short second branch is very important. It ensures that when the center brick button is pressed, `Mode Loop` is interrupted, allowing the EV3 to exit whichever operating mode is active and return to the menu so the user can select a new operating mode:

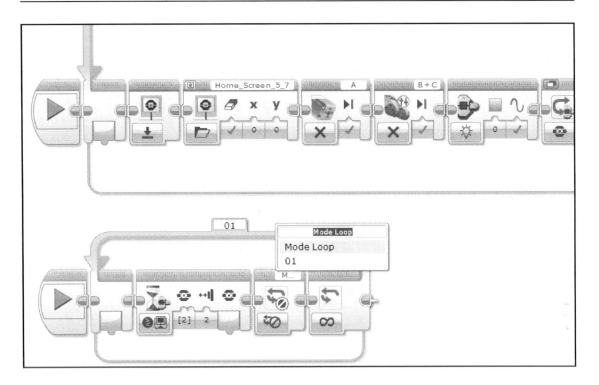

The completed GUI looks like this. Keep in mind that you can adapt this for any smart robot:

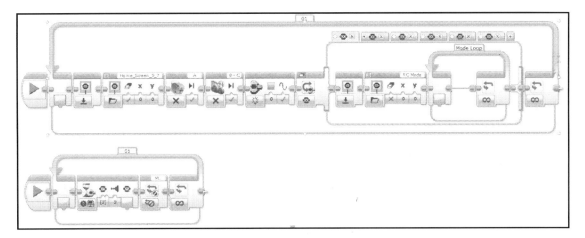

It is now time to fill that switch with code to make some fun operating modes!

Operating modes

We will start with the default blank case. If no brick buttons are pressed, no mode is active and the robot is idle. So, leave this case empty:

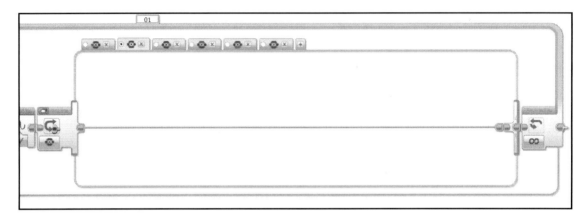

Remote control

Our first operating mode will be a review from the last chapter. **Remote Control** (**RC**) mode works exactly as the name implies; you can use the EV3 remote to control the Timmyton.

Within the `Mode Loop`, place the switch block and fill in the cases to make the RC mode. Note that the switch is in tabbed view mode to save space. We already covered programming tank-style RC in detail in the last chapter; since the RC programming for the Timmyton is largely the same, you can refer to the previous chapter for full instructions on how to program this. The only difference you will notice is that since the Timmyton's drive motors are placed in the conventional orientation, you do not need to negate the input power values; positive power will make the Timmyton drive forward:

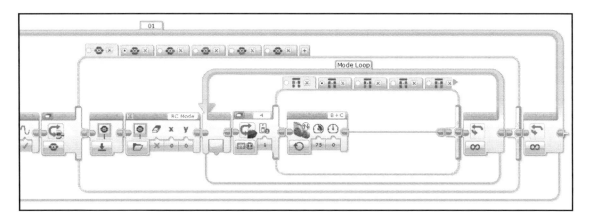

We will program the Timmyton to do something different when the top toggle button is pressed. Add a medium motor block (port A, **On**, power 100 percent) and a brick LED block. When the button is pressed, it will toggle the Timmyton's motorized jaws and tail and turn the brick LED red. Fit for a fearsome shark! (Recall from earlier in the chapter that the jaws and tail are designed so that continuous rotation of motor A will cause the two to continuously cycle.) The completed final case looks like this:

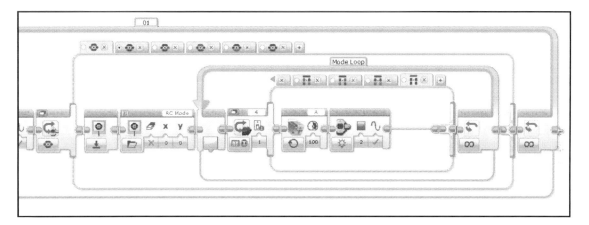

Jaws

Here is a fun operating mode, inspired by the famous movie of the same name. In this mode, the Timmyton will frantically move its jaws and tail, hunting down the infrared beacon while playing the infamous music! This is a beacon-seeking program, very similar to the one we made for the Security Tank.

Navigate over to the switch tab that has the right brick button highlighted. As usual, add the display reset and display print blocks at the beginning. Then, add a medium motor block (port A, **On**, 100 percent power). This motor block keeps the jaws and tail moving continuously while the operating mode is active:

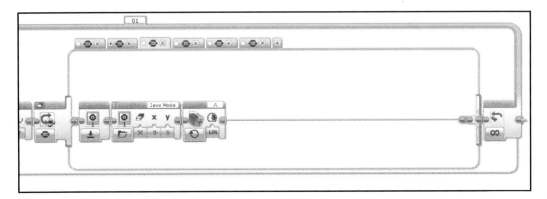

Now, it is time for something new: drag out two loops and place one under the other. Name both loops Mode Loop. Split the programming's flow so that it branches off to both loops. Drag the program's flow cable to create a new branch by clicking on the small tab on the right edge of the last block in the original branch, and drag the cable over to the first block in the new branch:

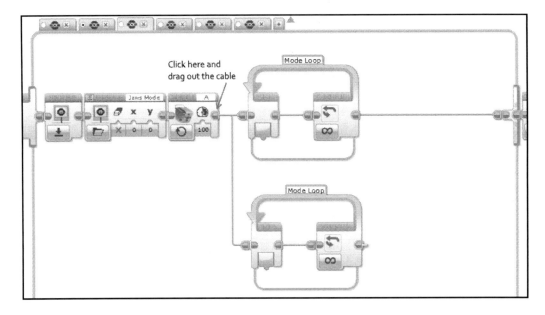

Program the beacon follower inside the top loop. You can follow the same steps we used to make the beacon follower for the Security Tank (refer back to `Chapter 2`, *Security Tank – Object-Tracking Robot*, for detailed instructions). Here, the beacon follower first checks for the presence of a nearby beacon using an IR sensor block and a logic switch.

If a beacon is present, the *true* case will activate and the robot will follow the beacon. The IR sensor will measure the beacon's heading and proximity and use them to adjust the robot's steering and power, respectively. The *k* value for the heading/steering control is `-2`, and the *k* value for the proximity/power control is `4`.

As you read through the *Mechanical design* section of this chapter, you may have noticed that the IR sensor is placed upside down. This was done to make mounting the sensor more convenient. We compensate for this in the program by making the *k* value for the Timmyton's heading/steering adjustment negative.

If no beacon is detected, the *false* case activates, which simply halts the drive motors and turns the brick LED orange:

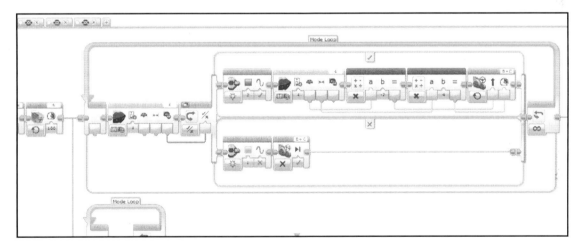

What about that second loop that we made? We will use it to run a second, smaller segment of code in parallel to the beacon tracking. This loop makes the Timmyton play a version of the ominous *Jaws* theme as it tracks the beacon. Place two sound blocks inside of the lower loop and set them both to **Play Note**. The first sound block will play a **C4** (lowest note) for a duration of `0.25` seconds, and the second block will play a **C#4** (half a step higher) for `0.3` seconds. This will repeat indefinitely while the Jaws mode is active, adding to the ominous mood while the Timmyton tracks its prey.

We also need to set the exit case for the lower loop to **Brick Buttons | Compare**. Set the middle brick button (button ID **2**) as the target button, and select action *2, pressed and released*. This is a redundant addition because of the loop exit branch we made when we set up the GUI earlier, but since Jaws mode has two branches running in parallel, the redundancy acts as a fail safe, adding an extra layer of security and ensuring the program runs smoothly without errors:

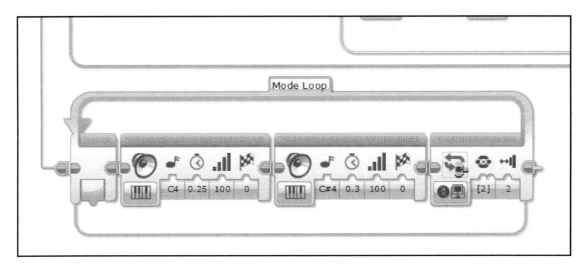

Hungry mode

Select the switch tab with the top brick button highlighted; it is time to program **Hungry** mode! In this mode, you can *feed* the Timmyton LEGO bricks. The color sensor in the mouth will recognize the color of the blocks, and the robot will react differently to each one.

You may notice that the switch block has expanded quite a bit. It will continue to expand as we add more programming. It will still be very large if you open up an empty switch case because it stretches to meet the size of the case with the largest program chunk and remains that size for all of the other cases.

Start by adding the typical blocks, plus a medium motor block (port A, **On for Rotations**, total of three rotations), placed directly before `Mode Loop`:

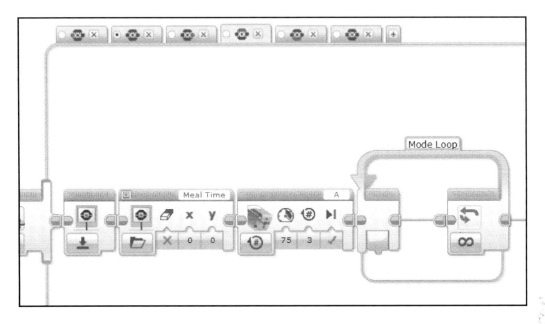

Set up a color sensor switch (port 3, **Color Sensor** | **Measure** | **Color**). Add four additional cases and assign each one to one of the following colors: no color, blue, green, yellow, red, and white. Set the *no color* case to the default case. This executes when no color blocks are detected by the color sensor. Leave this case empty:

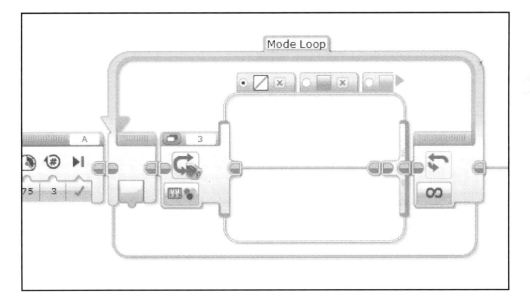

Now, we need to go through the rest of the switch cases and program the reaction that the Timmyton will have when it encounters each block. You have quite a bit of freedom to program the reactions, so get creative here! You can choose which color bricks the Timmyton likes to eat, which it will not eat, or think outside of the box! Each reaction starts with the Timmyton playing a sniffing sound and saying the color of the block. If the block is one of the preferred colors, the EV3 LED will light up green. If it is one of the colors the Timmyton dislikes, the brick LED will light up orange.

For reference, sample reactions are included here:

- **Blue**: One of the accepted colors. The Timmyton will say *okey-dokey* and chew on it for a second (running the jaws and tail while playing the crunching sound file):

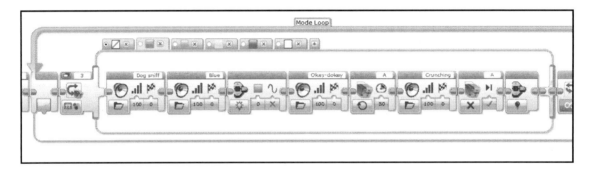

- **Green**: One of the colors the Timmyton dislikes. The robot will exclaim *Boo!*, then turn away quickly to reject the food:

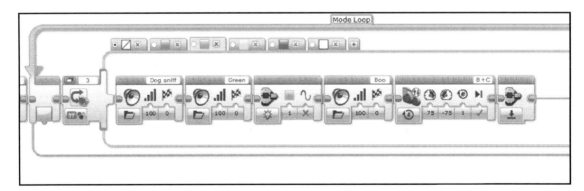

- **Yellow**: The second preferred color. The Timmyton will say *fantastic* and chew on it for a few seconds (very similar to its reaction to the blue block):

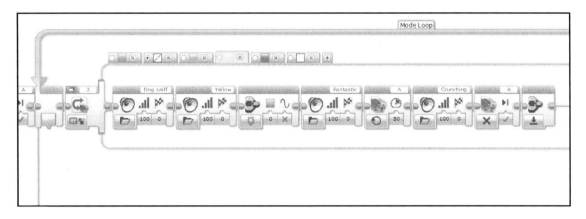

- **Red**: This will make the shark-like robot aggressive! The brick LED will light up red and the Timmyton will growl. Then, the shark will charge ahead at full speed for three seconds with its jaws and tail moving furiously:

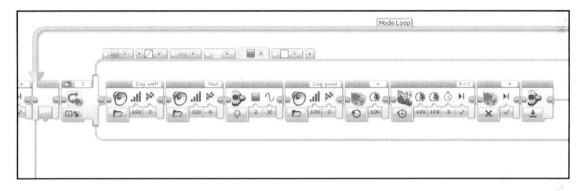

- **White**: This one causes the Timmyton to have an allergic reaction! The robot will exclaim *uh oh* and sneeze while twitching:

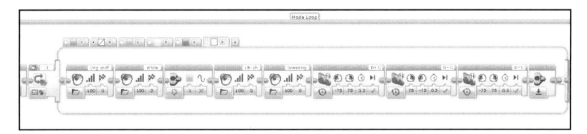

What kinds of creative reactions will you come up with?

Funky mode

In this mode, the Timmyton will play a simple dance tune while moving back and forth and flashing the brick LED in a multicolor pattern. Navigate to the switch tab with the bottom brick button highlighted. Then, set up this mode with the usual two display blocks, plus a wait with the duration set to 1 second, a medium motor block (port A, **On**, 100 percent power), and Mode Loop:

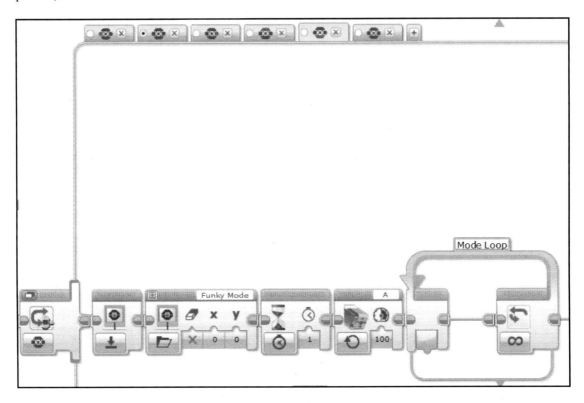

The programming for the dancing, music, and lights goes inside of Mode Loop. Fairly straightforward, right? Here is the program that gets the Timmyton to play and dance along to a simple waltz tune:

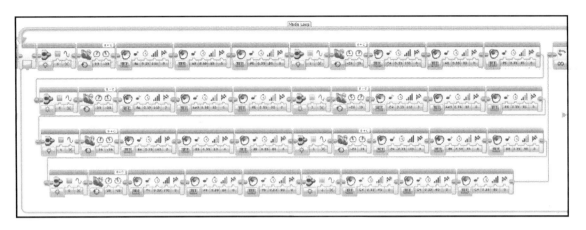

Yikes! The program itself is not too difficult, but because you need to program every individual note in the song and every corresponding action, this section of code ends up becoming very cumbersome. Note that there are four rows; the program flow moves from left to right across a row, and when the program flow comes to the end of a row, it proceeds to the beginning of the next row underneath. This saves space and makes the code section easier to read.

If you so choose, you can try this simpler alternative instead:

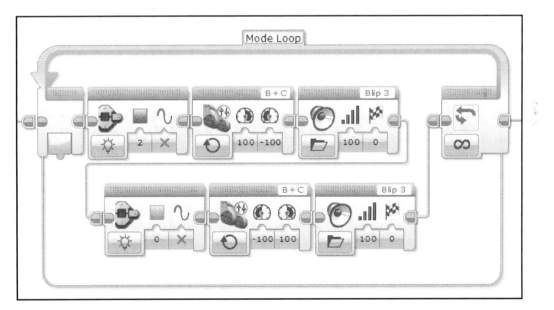

Autonomous

During autonomous mode, the Timmyton will roam around randomly until it encounters an object, then charge, stopping and turning around at the last second. This mode will be similar to the one we made for the Omnilander, but we will introduce some new concepts. Navigate over to the switch tab with the center brick button highlighted to program this final operating mode. Start filling in the switch case with the usual initialization blocks, plus a one second wait directly before Mode Loop:

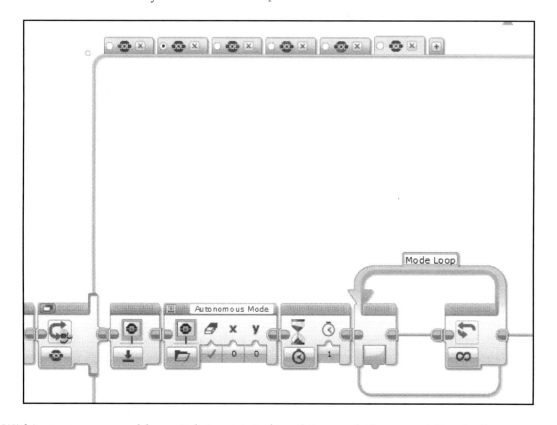

Within Mode Loop, add a switch (port 4, **Infrared Sensor** | **Compare** | **Proximity**, threshold value < | 35). This uses the IR sensor in the Timmyton's nose to check for nearby obstacles.

Then, program the *false* case. This executes when there are no obstacles nearby. The Timmyton will drive around randomly. First, the brick LED turns green. Then, to get a wandering effect when the Timmyton drives, we will add two random number blocks (from the *math* section). Set the minimum value to 1 and the maximum value to 100 for both of them. Add a move tank block after the random number blocks (**On**, **On for Seconds**, duration of 1 second). Then, plug the output of each random number block into one of the power inputs on the move tank block. This code will generate a random power value for each drive wheel and drive at these power levels for 1 second. Assuming that no obstacle comes into view, two new power values will be randomly generated, and the process repeats, giving the Timmyton's driving a wandering quality. When this code is finished, it looks like this:

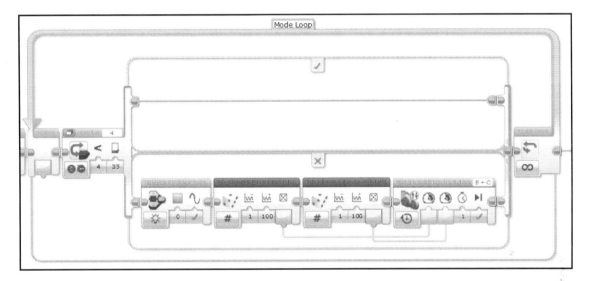

Now, we will program the *true* case, which executes when an object is present. The brick LED will turn red and the Timmyton will aggressively charge the obstacle with its chomping jaws and furious tail; program a medium motor block (port A, **On**, 100 percent power) and a move tank block (port B + C, **On**, both motors at 100 percent power). After that, place an infrared sensor switch (port 4, **Infrared Sensor** | **Compare** | **Proximity**, threshold value ≤ | 8). This switch checks to see if the Timmyton has moved closer to the object (if not, then it is no longer on track to collide with it):

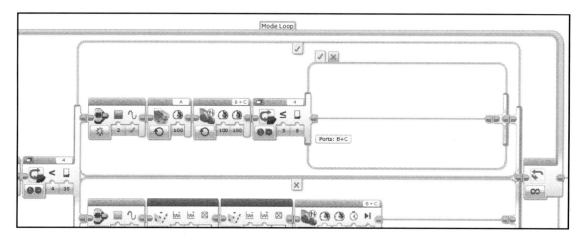

The *true* case of this switch executes when the Timmyton is very close to the object. The robot will stop its forward progress; drag out a medium motor block and a move tank block, setting both to the **Off** state. Two move tank blocks will follow, which will get the Timmyton to reverse, turn around, and continue in a new direction. The first block should be set to **On for Seconds** with both drive motors set to −75 percent power for a duration of 1 second. The second block should be set to **On for Degrees** with the left drive motor set to 75 percent power and the right motor set to −75 percent power for a duration of 1 second. After this, the Timmyton will continue in a new direction:

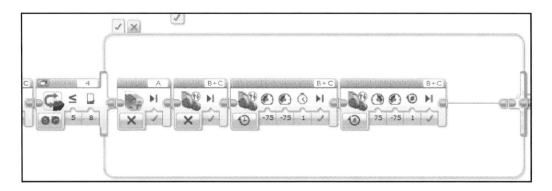

The *false* case of the switch executes if the Timmyton loses sight of the object while charging it. Inside the *false* case, place yet another IR sensor switch block (port 4, **Infrared Sensor** | **Compare** | **Proximity**, threshold value ≥ | 37). In the *true* case of this switch, insert a move tank block and a medium motor block, both set to **Off**:

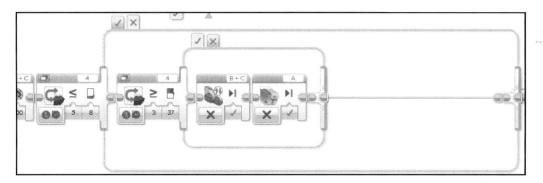

And for the *false* case? Just leave it blank, which tells the Timmyton to continue charging:

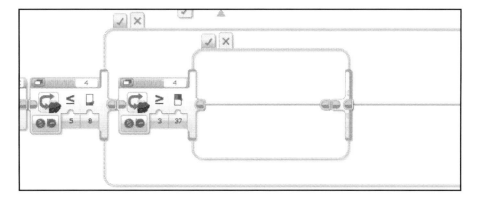

Putting it all together

Here is the completed program for the Timmyton. **Jaws Mode** is shown in the mode switch. Note that in this image, the music loop at the bottom-most branch of the Jaws mode program has been compressed into a MyBlock. We will learn about MyBlocks in Chapter 6, *Falcon – Remote Control Race Car*:

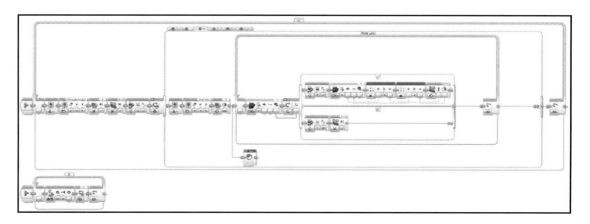

Give yourself a pat on the back, because you have just completed a very sophisticated EV3 program. Now, you can enjoy the fruits of your labor and show your new creation to your friends and family.

Summary

Wow, we learned a lot in this chapter! Let's review what we covered.

We started by introducing some cool new building techniques, such as creating a unique exterior design, using caster wheels for maximum mobility, and taking advantage of the bevel gear's ability to make both parallel and 90-degree gear meshes. Then, we revisited some of the engineering principles that we learned in earlier chapters, such as tank-style steering (this time with wheels) and cam-and-rod mechanisms.

We also expanded our knowledge of EV3 programming. We learned how to make a custom GUI, then incorporated the color sensor and the random number generator block for the first time. We reapplied beacon following, tank-style remote control, and obstacle detection/avoidance. Throughout the programming process, we saw some examples of how creative programming can give a robot its own unique personality!

Finally, we learned that a project may need multiple revisions before it is polished enough to be considered finished. In the case of the Timmyton, it took many revisions over the course of a few years to arrive at the completed robot. Keep this in mind when you are building your own smart robot; do not be discouraged if you need to redesign it!

By now, your library of EV3 knowledge is starting to become very deep. In the next chapter, we will be making another interactive robot, but taking things in a whole new direction. It is time to make Grunt, our first bipedal robot!

Grunt – Quirky Bipedal Robot

We have made three robots so far. By now, your library of robotics knowledge is becoming fairly deep. Now, it is time to try something more ambitious. Meet Grunt, an interactive robot that walks on two legs and has his own quirky personality! Grunt is a fictional alien character from a distant planet, with arms and legs like a human's, but with a dinosaur-like head and mouth.

When we build Grunt, we will be taking the mechanical design in a completely new direction. All of the robots we have made so far have used a tank-style drivetrain with either tracks or wheels to move around. Grunt does not rely on wheels to carry him around! Instead, he has a simple walking mechanism that allows him to shuffle around on two feet.

Like the Timmyton from the previous chapter, Grunt has several different operating modes that use his motors and sensors to create a fun interactive experience. The programming gives him a whimsical personality. However, when we program Grunt, we will be introducing a completely new technique. Where the Timmyton used a menu system to allow the user to select the different modes, Grunt's programming will streamline all of the modes into a simple AI-like program, so that the proper mode automatically activates based on a sensor state. All of the sensors continuously monitor the environment for a change that would prompt a specific operating mode to start. This type of program makes for an extremely smooth robot that is more lifelike than the Timmyton. Pretty smart, right?

Let's make a walking robot biped:

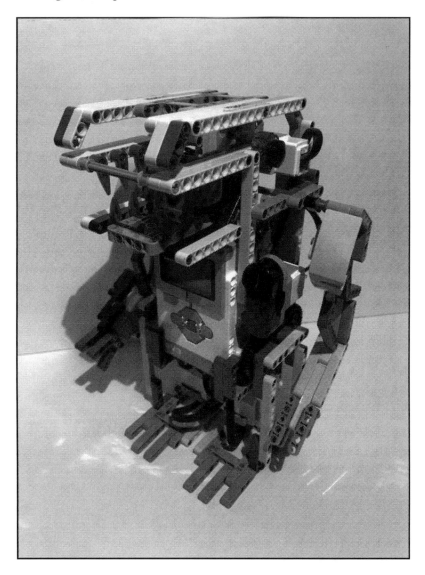

Technical requirements

You must have EV3 Home Edition Software V1.2.2 or newer installed on your computer. You may also install LEGO Digital Designer (LDD) V4.3 and download the LDD file for this project to guide you in the building process.

The LDD file is available on the **Downloads** page of the the Builderdude35 website:

`http://builderdude35.com/download/grunt-ldd/`

The LDD and EV3 files for this chapter are available on GitHub:

`https://github.com/PacktPublishing/Building-Smart-LEGO-MINDSTORMS-EV3-Robots/tree/master/Chapter05`

Check out this video to see the robot in action:

`https://goo.gl/basaqB`

Mechanical design

There are a lot of interesting techniques used in Grunt's design. We will take a glance at each one.

Walking mechanism

What makes Grunt stand out from all of the other projects in this book is that he does not use wheels or tank tracks to move around. Instead, he has a simple walking mechanism that allows him to move around on two legs.

Two EV3 large motors power the legs, one for each leg (ports B and C). Each motor directly drives a large 36-tooth bevel gear, which serves two purposes—it acts as a cam onto which one point of the leg is attached, and it transfers the motor's power through a 12-tooth gear to a second 36-tooth bevel gear, which acts as the second point on which the leg is attached. When the motor runs, the entire leg moves in a circular stepping motion. The two legs can move independently of one another:

Because these legs need to support the weight of the whole robot, each leg is reinforced using another beam, which attaches directly to the motor's red hub on the inside; it serves as the third attachment point for each leg, making for a robust mechanism:

The system comes together to allow Grunt to shuffle around. This type of walking is very slow and does not offer the much control, but considering that we made it with only two motors and a simple cam mechanism, the walking is acceptable. Making a smoother, more efficient walking mechanism requires many more motors and much more mechanical complexity. The shuffle-walk is sufficient for Grunt.

Cosmetic design

Grunt is another example of a robot whose visual appearance is very important to the robot as a whole. Grunt is a fictional creature from outer space, so appearance is a huge part of the robot's personality. Here are some features that help Grunt look the part:

First, Grunt has an alligator-shaped head, complete with a motorized mouth filled with sharp teeth. On either side of his head there is a bright blue eye, made using the round, translucent blue element found in the EV3 Expansion Set and a round black element.

Grunt stands upright and has an arm on either side of his torso, which gives him a human-like posture. The arms themselves are styled and detailed and even include three-fingered hands. The EV3 brick is located in the center of Grunt's torso, making it easily accessible.

Finally, the wide, sturdy legs end in flat feet that are complete with toes!

All of these design features come together to make a handsome robot that looks like a quirky alien creature:

Motorized functions

In addition to the two motors used for walking, Grunt includes two EV3 medium motors to animate a couple of other motorized features.

Mouth

An EV3 medium motor located in the back of Grunt's head (port D) opens and closes the mouth. The motor turns a cam-and-rod mechanism that is attached to the lower jaw. When the cam rotates forward, the rod pushes on the top of the lower jaw and the mouth opens; when the cam rotates in reverse, the rod pulls the mouth shut. Unlike the cams we used in our previous projects, this cam does not have continuous motion. Instead, it rotates 45 degrees to toggle the mouth between the open and closed positions:

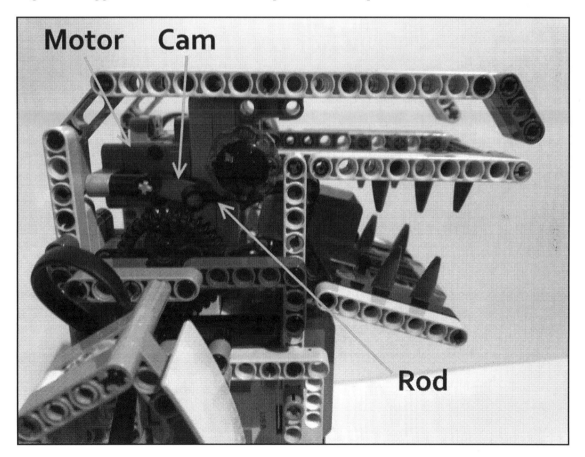

Arms

A second medium motor (port Λ) is located in the right side of Grunt's torso. This motor raises and lowers Grunt's arms. The motor is positioned vertically and sends its power to the right arm through a 90-degree gear connection that has a 3:1 gear ratio. The right arm is always mechanically fixed to this motor through this gear set:

This same motor powers the left arm as well. However, the left arm is not mechanically locked into the motor. Instead, a small clutch separates the half-shafts connected to each arm. The clutch is set up so that as the motor starts to move the right arm up, the left arm is disconnected and does not move. Once the right arm has moved halfway up, the clutch locks and the motor moves both the left and right arms.

If that was a little bit confusing, think of it this way: the right arm starts raising first and, when the right arm reaches the halfway point, the left arm starts to move up too.

The clutch was engineered into Grunt's arms because handshake mode requires that only the right arm moves, but other modes need both arms to move. Handshake mode does not need the arm to move up past the halfway point, but the other modes raise both arms all the way up. So, the clutch is a mechanical feature that satisfies both of these conditions without needing to use an independent motor for each arm:

A close-up LDD screenshot of the clutch gives us a clearer picture of how it works:

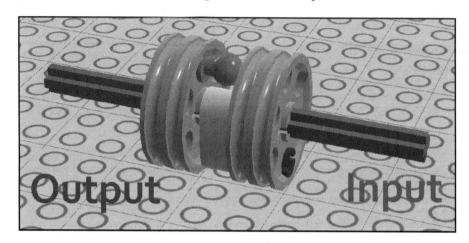

Some of the bricks are color-coded as a visual aid. The input (right) and output (left) are two separate axles that are not directly linked. The input is fixed to the motor, so it always rotates with the motor. The yellow block in-between the two plates is attached to the input shaft and rotates as the motor rotates. The green ball-shaped pin is attached to the output shaft. As the motor rotates the input shaft, the output shaft stays stationary until the yellow block rotates around and makes contact with the green pin. The yellow block pushes on the green pin as it continues to rotate, causing the output shaft to turn with the input shaft; the clutch is now locked and transfers the motor's rotation to the output shaft.

Since the clutch allows one motor to do the work of two and stays within the available materials (does not make the project exceed the EV3's limit of four motors), we can say that Grunt is equipped with some smart hardware!

Sensors

To create a smooth, interactive experience, Grunt makes use of three sensors that constantly monitor the environment to tell the robot which mode should be active: an infrared sensor, a color sensor, or a touch sensor.

Infrared sensor

Grunt's infrared sensor (port 4) is located on the left side of his torso and tucked away so that it does not alter his overall profile. The infrared sensor is primarily used as a proximity sensor to detect when a person comes near to trigger Grunt's greeting:

Color sensor

The color sensor (port 3) is located in Grunt's mouth. Like the Timmyton, when a LEGO block is placed in Grunt's mouth, the color sensor reads the color and Grunt reacts according to the color of the block:

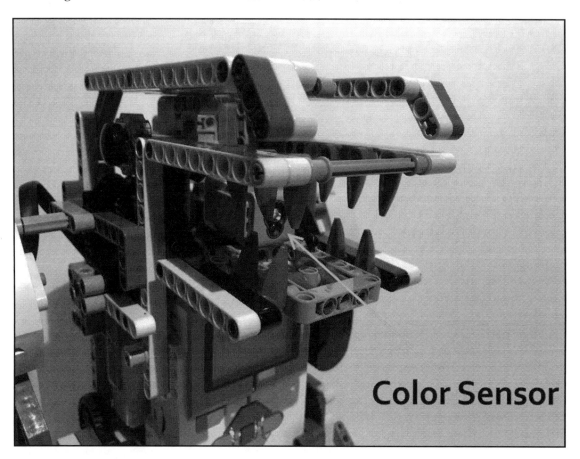

Touch sensor

This is a new sensor! The EV3 touch sensor is the simplest of all of the sensors. It has a button on the front and the sensor returns either one of two states: *true* if the button on the front of the sensor is pressed, or *false* if it is not pressed. This type of true/false logic is known as boolean logic.

Grunt's touch sensor is plugged into sensor port 1 and is located in his right arm. His right hand, which is made of red LEGO elements, is directly in front of the touch sensor. The hand is designed so that when Grunt's hand is squeezed, it presses the button on the front of the touch sensor, and the sensor returns a *true* value. A rubber band makes the hand open up again when the person lets go, and the sensor returns a *false* value. This feature is primarily used for Grunt's interactive handshake function:

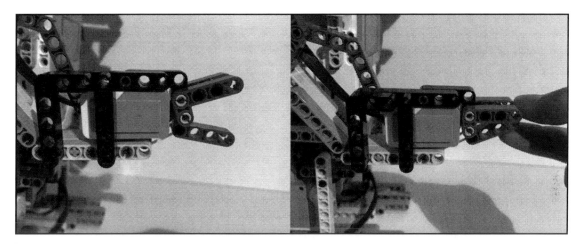

Now, we will find out how to program these sensors and hardware to make a cohesive, interactive robot!

Programming

Like the Timmyton, Grunt features one large program that incorporates all of his interactive features. However, where the Timmyton required the user to switch modes using a custom GUI, Grunt has a more sophisticated program that constantly monitors every sensor and automatically activates the corresponding mode. This allows Grunt to seamlessly transition between operating modes without user intervention, making him seem more lifelike. Let's find out how to make this special interactive program!

Setting up a simple AI

Because Grunt makes decisions autonomously and mimics an intelligent creature, we can consider his programming to be an example of a simple AI. This means that Grunt is the smartest robot we have made so far!

Recall from the last chapter that the Timmyton's program consisted of one main switch that activated an operating mode based on the brick button that was pressed. Grunt's method is more sophisticated. In order to imitate autonomous decision making, Grunt's programming relies on a series of nested switches. Each switch monitors a different sensor. If the sensor detects that a pre-defined parameter is met, then the corresponding mode will activate; if not, then the program continues down the line and checks the next sensor. If all of the switches return *false*, Grunt idles and the sensors are checked again.

 In the context of programming, nesting a switch refers to the practice of placing a switch within another switch. This is an efficient way to create a complex control system. Nesting many times will create a multi-tiered decision-making process for a robot. In Grunt's program, several switches are nested, with each checking a different parameter on one of the three sensors.

Now that we know about nesting, we can proceed to set up the framework for Grunt's decision-making program.

Initial code

Let's set up the first bits of code. Since Grunt will make use of the EV3 display to show information about the program's status, the first block to add is a reset for the EV3 display. Then, add a loop block, and set it to repeat infinitely. As with all of the other programs we have made so far, all further programming will be placed within the main loop.

We have two more blocks to place. Inside the loop, add a display block that prints No Mode to the EV3 display, which indicates that Grunt is idling. Then, add a block that changes the brick LEDs to green. Grunt will make use of the brick LEDs throughout the program to enhance the interactive experience, as well as indicate the status of the robot:

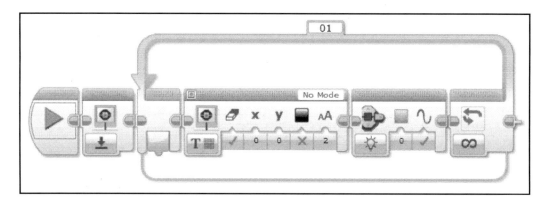

Nesting the switches

The first switch will check the status of the color sensor, which is used to activate hungry mode. Add a switch block and set it to **Color Sensor** | **Compare** | **Color** and verify that port 3 is selected. Then, define the set of colors as [1; 2; 3; 4; 5; 6; 7;]. This is every color that the EV3 color sensor can detect (black, blue, green, yellow, red, white, and brown, respectively). This means that whenever a LEGO brick of any color is placed into Grunt's mouth, the switch returns *true* and hungry mode automatically activates. Note that no color (ID **0**) is excluded. That is because if no color is detected, the switch will return *false* and the program will check the next sensor:

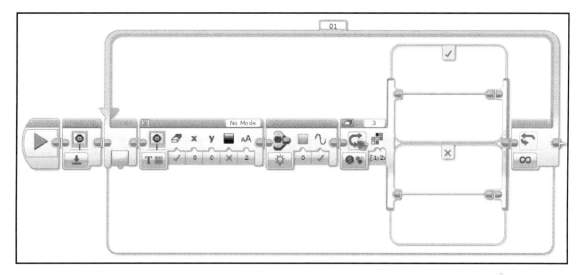

The code for the operating mode that corresponds with that sensor goes in the *true* case of each switch. We will leave the *true* cases alone for now; we are setting up the skeleton for the AI first. In the next section, we will return and fill in the switches with code for the operating modes.

In the *false* case, we will place another switch, which checks the next sensor; this is where the nesting starts. The second switch should be set to **Infrared Sensor** | **Compare** | **Proximity**, the threshold value will be less than or equal to 30, and the sensor port will be 4. This switch uses the IR to check if there is a person nearby; if so, then handshake mode activates. If not, then the program checks the next sensor.

Your first nested switch will look like this:

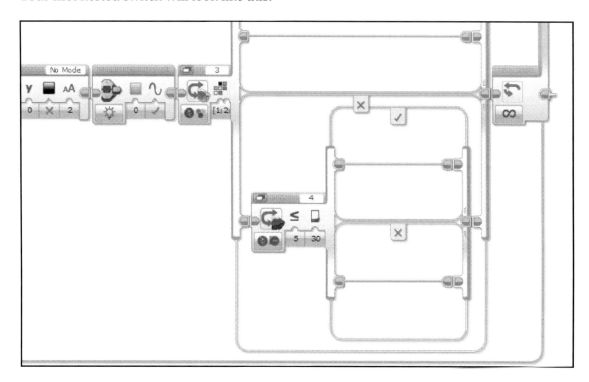

The next nested switch will also check the IR sensor, but this time the IR sensor is in infrared receiver mode. This switch activates RC mode, Grunt's remote control feature. The switch should be set up as follows: **Infrared Sensor** | **Compare** | **Remote**, port 4, remote channel 1. The set of remote button ID's should be: [1; 2; 3; 4; 5; 6; 7; 8; 9;]. This is similar to what we did for the color sensor switch; we chose almost all of the button IDs so that RC mode activates when almost any button combination is pressed on the remote. Note that we have not included ID **10** and **11**; these are reserved because they are used to exit RC mode. We will use them later:

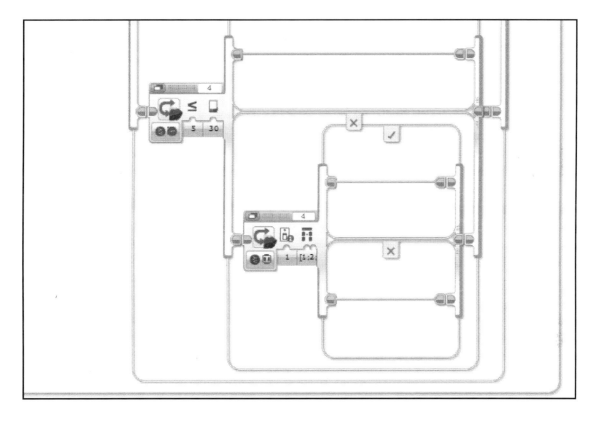

Now, place another switch within the *false* case of the previous one. This one monitors the state of the middle button on the EV3 brick and activates Grunt's Tantrum mode. The switch should be set to: **Brick Buttons** | **Measure**. (Note that this is the only switch that is in measure mode as opposed to compare mode.) Select button ID **2** (center button) for the top case, and button ID **0** (no button) for the bottom case. Then, set the bottom case as the default case. The completed switch for the brick buttons will look like this:

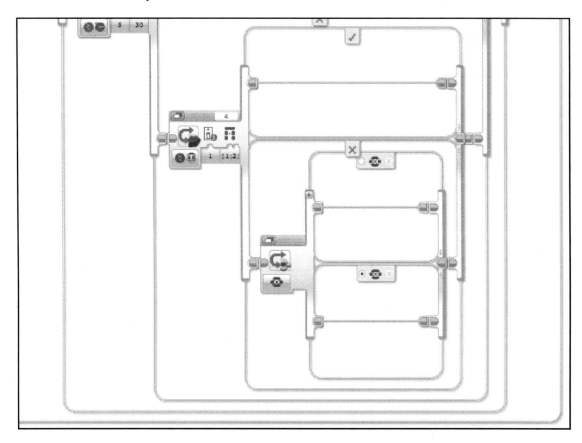

Finally, we have just one more switch left to nest! This switch monitors the touch sensor and provides an alternative way to activate handshake mode, in which the user initiates the handshake. Set the switch to **Touch Sensor** | **Compare** | **State**, select **State 1** (sensor pressed), and select port 1. This is the first time we have programmed the touch sensor, but, as you can see, it is a very straightforward sensor. When the sensor is pressed, the switch returns *true* and handshake mode activates; if the sensor is not pressed, the switch returns *false*:

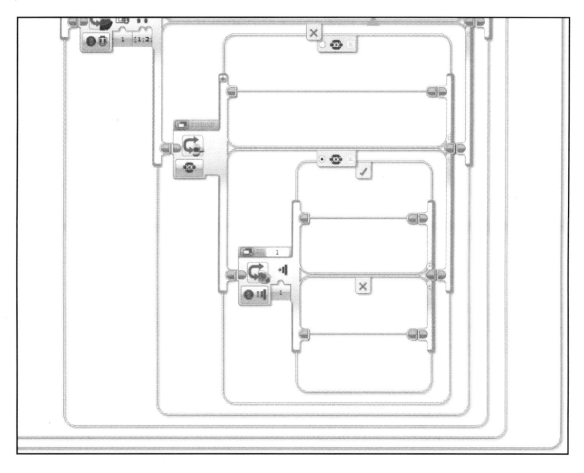

We have finished nesting the switches, which provides us with the generic skeleton for an AI program. If you make a smart robot that has a tiered decision-making process, you can adapt this code and add, subtract, and edit the switches and their assigned sensors.

The order in which Grunt's program checks the sensors was chosen because it minimizes the chance that the switches will interfere with one another and cause the program to fail. Make sure that you consider this when you adapt this code for your own smart robot.

Programming the modes

Now that we have the program's decision-making logic complete, we can start to fill in the switches with code for the operating modes.

Hungry mode

This mode is a review of the Hungry mode we programmed for the Timmyton in the last chapter, as it is fairly similar. The code for this mode will go inside the *true* case of the color sensor switch.

The first few blocks will initialize the operating mode. Add a display block that prints `Hungry Mode` to the EV3 screen, a brick LED block that shuts the LED's off, and a switch (**Color Sensor** | **Measure** | **Color**, port 3). After the switch, place a move tank block that turns motors `B` and `C` off:

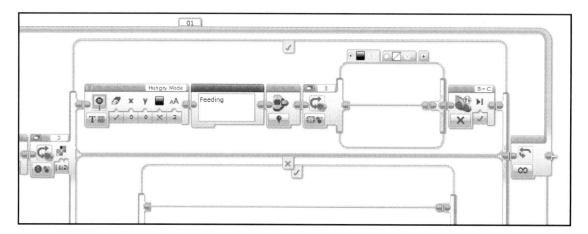

But wait, what is that blue block after the display block? That is a comment. What does it do? Nothing! That's right. Comments are a way for a programmer to leave notes within a program and they do not affect the way that the robot executes the code. Comments are extremely useful because they can store information about what the program is doing at that point. Here, a comment is used as a label to indicate that this is the section of the program that controls Hungry mode. Using comments is not only a good programming habit, but it becomes increasingly important as the program becomes more complex. In a text-based programming language such as C, Python, or Java, a comment can even be used to temporarily remove a section of code, which makes them a great tool for debugging!

Use comments throughout your code; they will not only make your program easier to navigate, but will also help someone who is not familiar with your code understand it more easily. Commenting code is a practice used by the most successful professional programmers, so start getting into the habit of adding them today!

Now, we should set up that switch. Add a few more cases and assign each case to a color that you want Grunt to react to. Make sure that you also include a null case that executes when no color is detected and make it the default case:

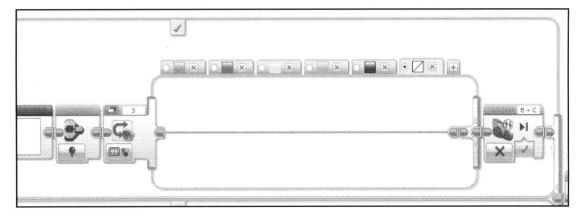

Inside each of the switch cases, we will program Grunt's reaction to the assigned color. You have a lot of freedom to program some creative reactions to the different color blocks the user may feed him.

Here are some sample reactions Grunt can respond with when fed a certain color. Each time he is fed a block, the brick LED lights up to indicate whether he likes the food, he says the color of the block, and he reacts.

If he is fed a blue block (a type of food he likes), the brick LED will turn green and Grunt will express his approval by saying the color name and saying *Mmmm*, then make a crunching sound while he chews on it for a few seconds. The loop block moves his jaws to simulate a chewing effect. Then, he opens his mouth to let the block drop out in anticipation for the next block of food and closes his mouth:

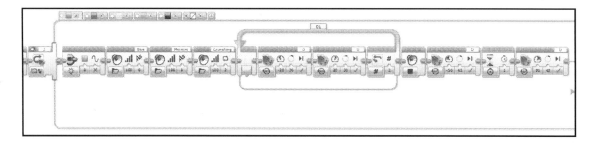

 Note that Hungry mode uses some custom sound files, which were made using the Sound Editor within the EV3 programming environment. The Sound Editor is found in the **Tools** menu. Using the Sound Editor is fairly straightforward; it allows you to record, import, and edit sounds, then save them for use in your project.

Red is another type of food that Grunt enjoys eating. If presented with a red block, he will exclaim *Yum!*, and react in a similar manner:

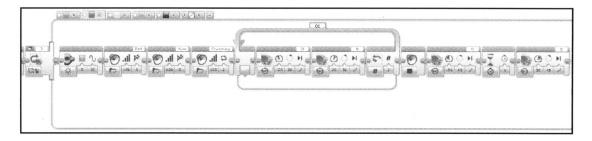

Grunt does not like yellow blocks! If he is fed one, the brick LED's will light up orange, and he will express his disapproval by spitting the block out:

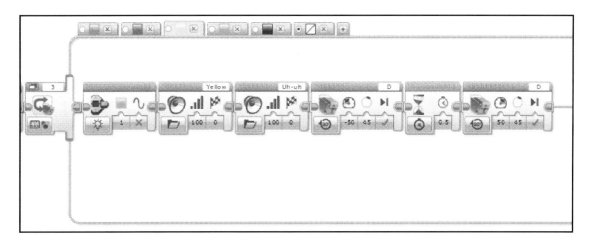

Grunt also dislikes green foods and will reject them in a similar fashion:

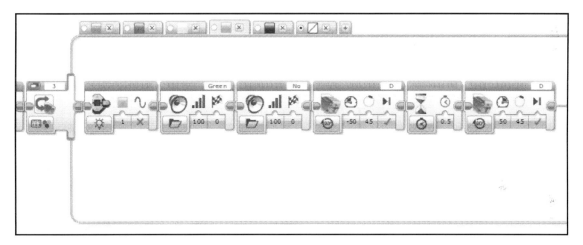

A brown block elicits the most interesting reaction! The brick LEDs will light up red, and Grunt will groan with an *Ugh*. Then, he will go berserk: he will throw both arms into the air, open his mouth, and aggressively shuffle around:

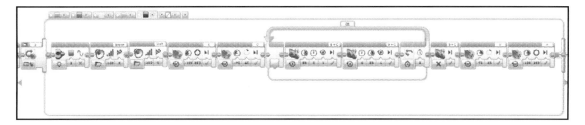

Finally, we have the null case, which tells Grunt to do nothing when no block is present in his mouth. It is somewhat redundant, but it acts as a fail-safe that keeps the program running smoothly:

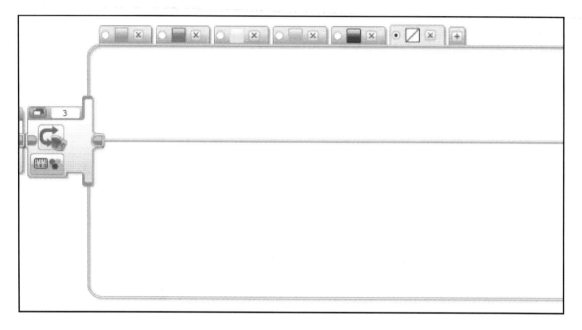

Handshake

If Grunt's IR sensor detects a nearby person, he will greet the person by extending his arm and offering a handshake. He will hold his arm out for three seconds. If the person accepts the offer, the touch sensor in Grunt's hand will detect that the person is squeezing his hand, and he will shake his or her hand. If the three seconds expire and the person has not shaken Grunt's hand, he will put it back down. This is another example of a novel interactive feature that lends Grunt a rich interactive experience.

The first step in programming the handshake sequence is to add the usual initialization code: a display block that prints Handshake to the EV3 screen and a block that changes the brick LEDs to orange. You may also wish to incorporate a comment to label the programming sequence for later reference:

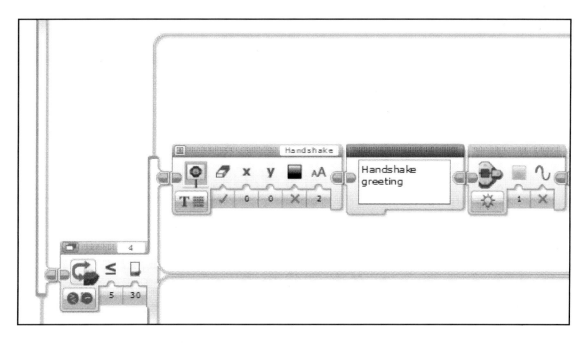

The next step is to add a medium motor block (**On for Degrees**, -100 percent power, 150 degrees, port A), which makes Grunt raise his arm halfway to offer a handshake (this is where the clutch mechanism we mentioned earlier comes in handy). Then, Grunt will introduce himself by playing a custom sound file. After that, place a loop and set it to repeat for three seconds; name this loop Handshake. The loop makes Grunt wait three seconds for the person to return his greeting:

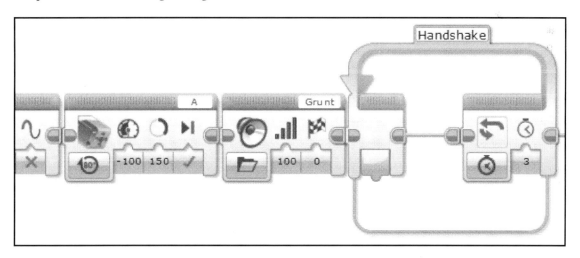

Now, we will program inside the loop. Add a switch block (**Touch Sensor** | **Compare** | **State**, state 1, port 1) and activate tabbed view. This switch checks to see if Grunt's hand is currently being squeezed. If so, he will finish the handshake. In the *true* case of the switch, place a block that turns the brick LED's green to affirm that the handshake has been accepted.

Then, add another loop, and set it to repeat for five counts. Place two medium motor blocks within the new loop. The first motor block should be set to **On for Degrees**, 65 percent power, 75 degrees, port A; the second should be set to **On for Degrees**, −65 percent power, 75 degrees, port A. When the loop executes, Grunt will move his right arm up and down several times to make a handshaking motion.

Immediately after the loop (but still within the *true* case of the touch sensor switch), place a loop interrupt block and program it to interrupt the handshake loop. Once Grunt has completed the handshake, this block will end Grunt's three second wait:

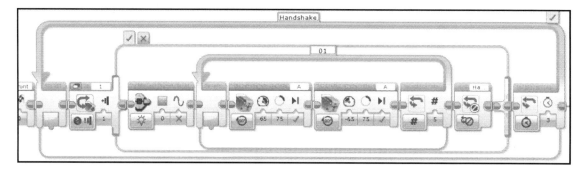

There is no programming in the *false* case of the touch sensor switch; if the touch sensor does not detect that Grunt's hand is being squeezed, he will simply continue to wait.

The last block in the handshake sequence returns Grunt's arm back to its resting position. This is accomplished using a medium motor block (**On for Degrees**, 50 percent power, 150 degrees, port A):

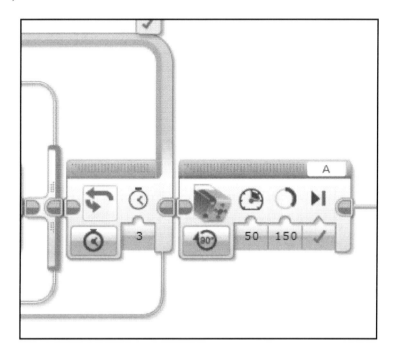

Remote control

As the name implies, this mode allows the user to control Grunt using an EV3 remote. The programming for this mode goes within the *true* case of the second IR sensor switch.

Start by adding a display block that prints **RC Mode** to the EV3 brick's screen. Adding a comment as a label would be helpful. Then, add a loop block. Set the exit case for the loop to: **Infrared Sensor** | **Compare** | **Remote**, channel 1, port 4. Then, select button IDs **10** and **11**. These are the button combinations that we reserved earlier; they are being used to exit the remote control loop. Finally, be sure to name the loop RC:

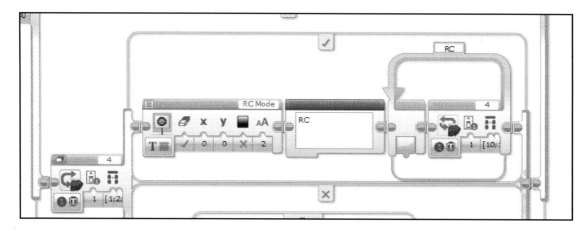

Place a switch inside the RCloop. The switch should be set to: **Infrared Sensor** | **Measure** | **Remote**, channel 1, port 4. Then, add additional cases and assign each to a different button combination that you would like to use to control Grunt. Make sure that you do not use either button ID **10** or **11**, as these are reserved for exiting the loop. Make the null case (no buttons pressed) the default case and place a move tank block within it that will stop the walking motors:

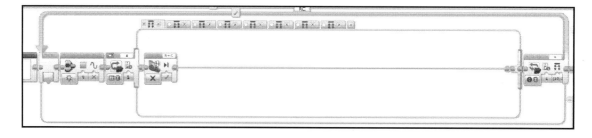

Then, you can start filling in each case with programming that controls Grunt's legs according to the button combination on the remote. Individually explaining how to program each case would take too long, but there are some guidelines you can follow: 85 percent is the optimal power level for stepping, and a negative power makes Grunt step forward. For the best walking motion, use a move tank block that moves each leg individually for one full rotation.

For example, here is the code to make Grunt's left leg step forward to make him shuffle a right turn:

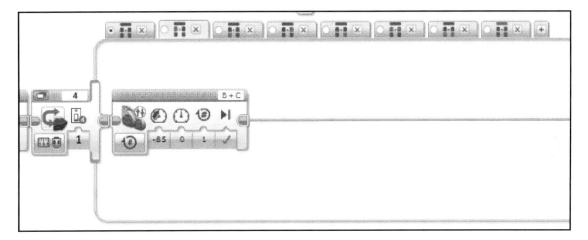

This is how you would program him to walk forward; note that each leg moves individually for one rotation:

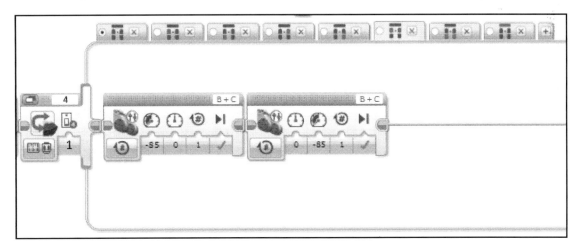

You may wish to use the top button to activate Grunt's Tantrum sequence. We will cover how to program this in the next section. Since the top button is a toggle switch, you need to add a loop interrupt block at the end of the code in this case and set the block to end the RC loop. This will prevent the sequence from repeating itself:

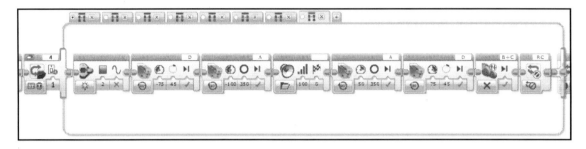

Tantrum

If the center button on the EV3 brick is pressed, Grunt will throw up his arms, stomp around, and roar in a fit of rage. The Tantrum sequence will be programmed within the *true* case of the brick button switch. We start with the usual setup code, a Display block and a Brick LED block:

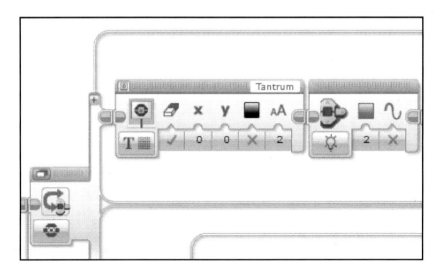

Next, Grunt will throw his arms above his head. Add a medium motor block (**On for Degrees**, -100 percent power, 350 degrees, port A). A second medium motor block (**On for Degrees**, -75 percent power, 45 degrees, port D) will open his mouth. A sound block will play a custom sound file and make him emit a mighty roar:

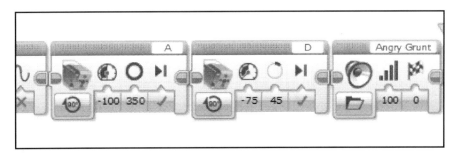

Then, drag out a loop block; set it to repeat for five counts and name it Angry. Place two move tank blocks within the loop. The first move tank block should be set to **On for Rotations**, motor B: -85 percent power, motor C: 0 percent power, 1 rotation. The second will be set the same way as the first, but with the left/right power levels split (**On for Rotations**, motor B: 0 percent power, motor C: -85 percent power, 1 rotation). This bit of code will make Grunt stomp around for a few seconds:

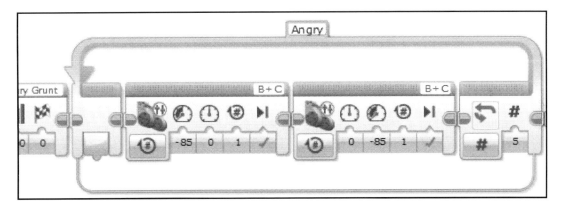

After Grunt has finished his fit of rage, he calms down and returns to his resting position. Each of the motors resets to its original position. The first medium motor block (**On for Degrees**, 75 percent power, 45 degrees, port D) returns his mouth to the closed position, while the second medium motor block (**On for Degrees**, 100 percent power, 350 degrees, port A) brings his arms back to his sides. Finally, a move tank block (**Off**) halts the two leg motors, bringing him to a stop:

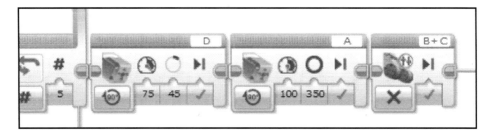

Handshake – alternative trigger

The final switch in the sequence is the touch sensor switch. It is an alternative way to trigger the handshake sequence. This feature allows the user to initiate the handshake, to which Grunt will respond by running the handshake sequence:

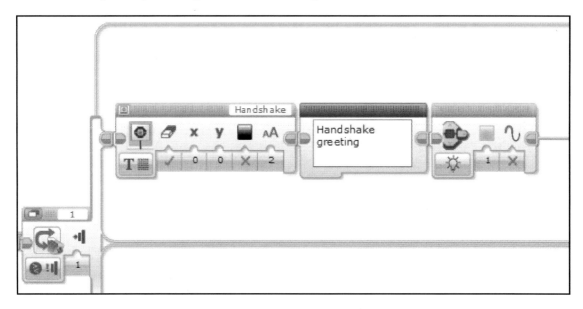

The programming in this switch is the same exact handshake sequence we made earlier. Refer back to that section for more detailed instructions on how to program it:

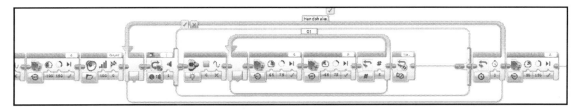

Null case

The null case is the *false* case of the touch sensor switch (the final switch in the sequence). This case executes if none of the sensors have detected any of the desired parameters. No modes have activated, so Grunt simply stands idle, checks the sensors again, and waits until one of the parameters is met:

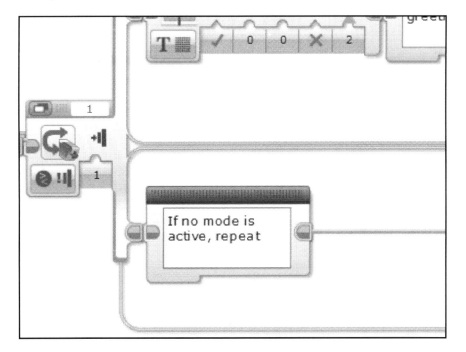

Putting it all together

There you have it, Grunt's completed program! Looking at the program as a whole shows how all of the nested switches interact with each other. It also gives us a clearer idea of the scale of this program:

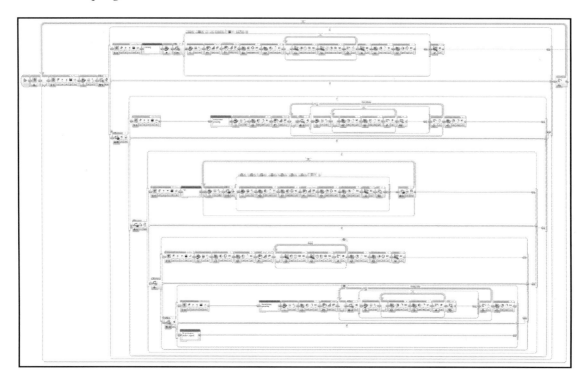

While this program is very complex for an EV3 robot, it is a very rewarding program to make because it offers a rich interactive experience and is a great example of how real-world smart robots use nested switches to make complex decisions. The program itself is an example of a very simple AI! The sophisticated decision-making and pre-programmed reactions come together to create a cohesive, lifelike robot with a quirky personality.

Summary

We just completed our most complex EV3 robot so far! Let's review what we have learned.

Being a bipedal robot, Grunt was our first departure from tank-style locomotion. We made a robot that walks instead of drives and learned about the simple walking mechanism that allows Grunt to shuffle about. Next, we discussed some of the aspects of the exterior design that help develop Grunt's character and give him the appearance of an alien creature from a distant planet. We revisited cams and gear ratios, then introduced a completely new mechanism, a clutch-like locking axle; Grunt's mechanical design demonstrates the usefulness of this mechanism for creating two different motions, one delayed behind the other, using only one motor. This is a great concept to have in your toolkit when you design your own smart robot.

We made our most sophisticated program yet, a simple AI that continuously reads all of its sensors and seamlessly switches to the proper operating mode to give Grunt a lifelike appearance and simulate intelligent behavior. We learned about nesting, the practice of placing a switch inside of a switch, and discussed the advantages of adding comments to our code. We introduced a new sensor, the touch sensor. Finally, we saw how creative programming features (such as custom sounds, LED lights, interactive motors, and so on) can come together to give a robot a fun personality!

Grunt is the smartest robot we have made yet! In the next chapter, we will learn about some smart hardware and how a robot can have intelligence, even in a remote control program, when we make the Falcon race car.

Falcon – Remote Control Race Car

6

So far, we have made a few robots that used tank-style steering, and one walking bipedal robot. In this chapter, we will be doing something completely new: we are going to build the Falcon, a remote control car! The steering method for the Falcon, conveniently referred to as car steering, is different from anything we have seen so far. We will also learn about the car-style drivetrain and relate it to the mechanisms used by cars in the real world. We will specifically look at how the Falcon's drivetrain gives it the speed and agility of a race car.

It may seem strange to include a remote control car in a book about smart robots. A smart robot must, by definition, make decisions about the environment and react accordingly. So, if a human controls the robot with a remote, how can this robot be considered smart? You will soon see that programming for the car-style steering used in the Falcon is quite intelligent. The steering must constantly monitor its own position using the rotation sensor, and automatically return to center. Even though the user gives the Falcon a command, the EV3 must coordinate a few different actions and monitor the status of the sensors to successfully carry out the command. Additionally, the Falcon uses some special smart hardware that enables it to steer like a car. Because of its intelligent hardware and software, the Falcon can still be considered smart, even though a human controls it with a remote.

We will now take a look at how this sleek speed machine works:

Technical requirements

You must have EV3 Home Edition Software V1.2.2 or newer installed on your computer. You may also install LEGO Digital Designer (LDD) V4.3 and download the LDD file for this project to guide you in the building process.

The LDD file is available on the **Downloads** page of the the Builderdude35 website:

http://builderdude35.com/download/falcon-ldd/

The LDD and EV3 files for this chapter are available on GitHub:

https://github.com/PacktPublishing/Building-Smart-LEGO-MINDSTORMS-EV3-Robots/
tree/master/Chapter06

Check out this video to see the robot in action:

https://goo.gl/9FL3HL

Mechanical design

The Falcon features a unique mechanical design that is similar to the designs used by some cars in the real world. This smart hardware makes the Falcon's driving fast and smooth.

The drivetrain and steering in the Falcon are completely different from anything that we have discussed in this book thus far. In the previous chapters, we made robots that used tank-style driving, where two EV3 large motors powered the robot. In these systems, each large motor was dedicated to the wheels or tracks on one side of the robot. This system used direct drive, meaning that the drive motor was directly connected to the wheel/track without any gears or other mechanisms in between. The robot steered by varying the power split between the two motors.

The Falcon changes all of this. In fact, the only similarity that the Falcon's drivetrain shares with those previous robots is that it is powered by two EV3 large motors. In the Falcon, or any car-style drive system, power and steering are separate functions. This means that the drive motors are used to propel the robot forward while a separate motor steers the car's front wheels. This is different from tank-style steering, in which the drive motors handle both power and steering simultaneously.

Because the driving and steering mechanisms in the Falcon are independent of one another, we will discuss them in separate sections. We will also examine the visual design and the sensors used.

Drivetrain

The Falcon's drivetrain uses quite a few moving parts, and is a simplified version of the system that you may find in a real car. The Falcon's drivetrain is classified as **rear-wheel drive (RWD)** because the power to propel the car is transferred to the ground through the rear wheels. This is the simplest setup because the rear wheels are dedicated to driving and the front wheels are dedicated to steering. Front-wheel drive and all-wheel drive systems are commonly used in real-world cars as well, but require more complex drive systems.

Drive motors

The most logical way to understand the Falcon's drivetrain is to walk through it in the same order that the torque is transferred from the motors to the wheels. The two EV3 large motors (ports B and C) located in the rear of the car provide the power to propel the Falcon. They are hard-coupled, meaning that they are fixed together with a solid axle and always rotate with the same speed and direction.

The two drive motors and most of the drivetrain are visible after removing the EV3 brick:

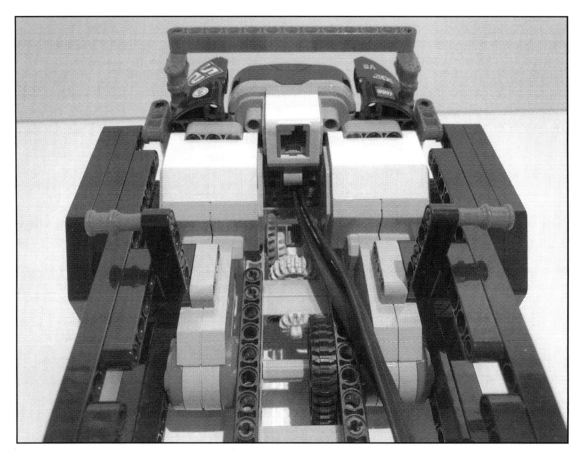

Gear ratios

The two drive motors transfer their power through a 90-degree gear set that has a 1:3 gear ratio. In previous chapters, we used gear ratios to give the motors a mechanical advantage and multiply their torque at the expense of speed. Now, we are doing the opposite; the Falcon uses this gear set to multiply the drive motors' output RPM by a factor of three, while sacrificing torque. This gear setup was chosen because it allows the Falcon to reach a higher top speed. We can do this at the expense of torque because the two EV3 large motors supply enough torque to drive the car, even with the taller gear ratio.

The 90-degree gear set redirects the motors' torque through a short axle that runs lengthwise. This short driveshaft in turn transfers the torque to the rear axle.

 In the context of a car, an axle that runs in the direction of the car's length (front/rear axis) is referred to as longitudinal. An axle that runs in the direction of the car's width (left/right) axis is referred to as latitudinal or transverse.

Differential

There is another 90-degree gear connection on the rear axle, which transfers the torque from the short longitudinal driveshaft to the latitudinal rear axle. However, this is not an ordinary gear connection; this is a special type of mechanism called a differential:

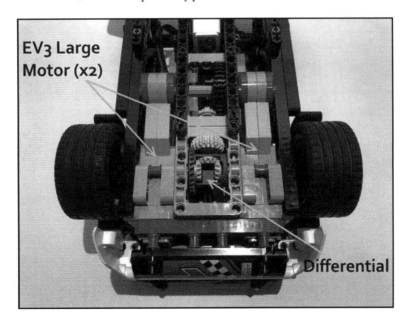

What does a differential do? First, it is important to understand one of the fundamental issues of the car-style drive system. When a car steers, it makes a wide, arcing turn, in which the outside wheels travel more distance than the inside wheels. Therefore, the outside wheels must drive faster to compensate for the increased distance they travel. If the drive wheels are connected by a solid axle, the engine will supply both wheels with the same amount of torque at all times. This means that both drive wheels will always rotate at the same speed, which is an issue because the car will resist turning.

The differential solves this problem by allowing the two drive wheels to spin at different speeds while the motors power them. A pinion gear (in this case, the sand-colored 20-tooth bevel gear) transfers power to the large ring gear on the grey differential housing. This type of 90-degree setup is called a ring-and-pinion gear set.

There are three small sand-colored conical gears inside the differential housing. Each of the rear wheels is connected to its own half of the rear axle; the two halves are semi-independent of one another, but linked together through the gear mesh between these three gears. The right conical gear is directly connected to the right half of the rear axle, the left conical gear is connected to the left half, and the center conical gear is mounted directly on the differential housing. The center gear is able to rotate freely while moving with the differential housing, which is what allows the differential to change the rotation speed of each half of the rear axle to meet the speeds necessary to make the turn.

There are different types of differentials. The type used here is called an open differential because it allows the two halves of the axle to rotate and change speed freely. This is the simplest type of differential, but the disadvantage is that if one wheel gets stuck or lifts off the ground, the torque will always take the path of least resistance and the car will become stranded. A limited-slip differential solves this issue, but is more complicated. Because the Falcon typically keeps all of its wheels planted firmly on the ground at all times, an open differential is sufficient.

The differential is an excellent piece of smart hardware that is used in real-world cars because it adds a passive intelligence to the drivetrain by varying the torque sent to each wheel to allow for smooth turning. After the differential, the torque makes it to each of the rear wheels through their respective halves of the rear axle, allowing the Falcon to drive.

Final drive ratio

The final drive ratio of a drivetrain describes the overall gear ratio of the entire drivetrain from the first input to the final output. In the context of the Falcon, it describes the overall gear ratio between the drive motors and the rear wheels. The final drive ratio is useful because while there may be many different gear sets with varying ratios within one drivetrain, it gives us a, big picture, look at the mechanism as a whole.

To calculate the final drive ratio, simply multiply the gear ratio of each individual gear set together. In the Falcon, there are two gear sets that change the rotation speed. The first is the 90-degree set that comes directly from the drive motors, with a ratio of 1:3. The second is the ring-and-pinion gear set on the differential. The 20-tooth pinion drives the 28-tooth ring to make a gear ratio of 1.4:1, which can also be expressed in decimal form as 0.714. Multiplying 3 by 0.714 yields the Falcon's final drive ratio of 1:2.142. This ratio indicates that for each time the drive motors complete one rotation, the rear wheels rotate 2.142 times.

Steering

The Falcon uses a steering mechanism that is similar to the mechanism used in real world cars. Steering is accomplished using a steering rack that pivots the front wheels to the right or left. One EV3 medium motor (port A) controls the steering:

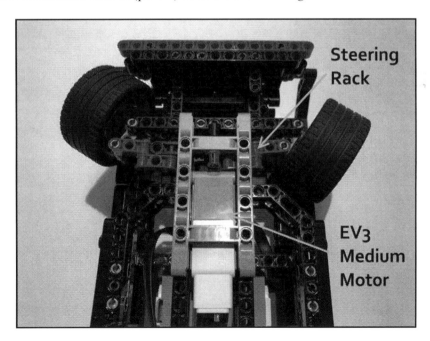

A rack-and-pinion mechanism is used to steer the Falcon's front wheels. This also happens to be the most common method of steering used in real-world cars. We first introduced rack-and-pinion when we made the Omnilander. Recall that it uses a circular gear (the pinion) to slide a long toothed bar (the rack) from side to side. A rack-and-pinion mechanism is a type of linear actuator because it converts rotary motion to linear motion. In the Falcon, this linear motion is used to push or pull the lever on which each of the front axles is attached, causing the front wheels to pivot in one direction to steer the car.

The rack-and-pinion steering mechanism is visible when the medium motor and some cosmetic panels are removed:

Later in the chapter, we will discuss the programming that coordinates this steering mechanism to make smooth, car-like steering that returns to center.

Cosmetic design

Like the Timmyton and Grunt, visual appearance was an important design consideration when building the Falcon. Elements of the Falcon's exterior design work together to give the car a sleek appearance and hint at its capacity for speed, even before it moves.

The front of the car is covered with flat panels to give the car a smooth profile. The wheels are housed within wide fenders to give the Falcon the appearance of a true race car:

Special consideration was also given to the rear of the vehicle, where red stripes run down either side from the roof, and wrap around the back at the spoiler. Wide fenders frame the rear wheels, and the stylish rear bumper boasts an aggressive-looking diffuser.

Finally, the EV3 brick is positioned atop the car in a way that allows for easy access while staying within the car's sporty profile:

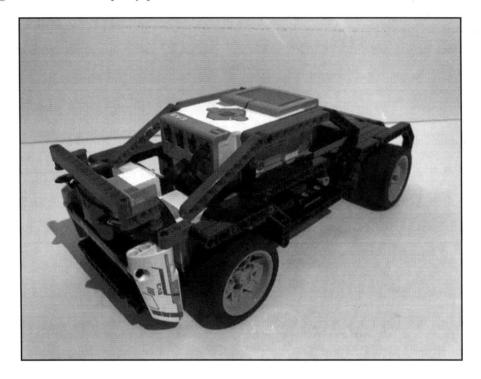

Sensors

The Falcon uses two sensors to coordinate its driving, the infrared sensor and the rotation sensor.

Infrared sensor

The infrared sensor (port 4) is located in the back of the vehicle, streamlined into the design of the rear bumper. It functions as an infrared receiver for the commands sent from the EV3 remote.

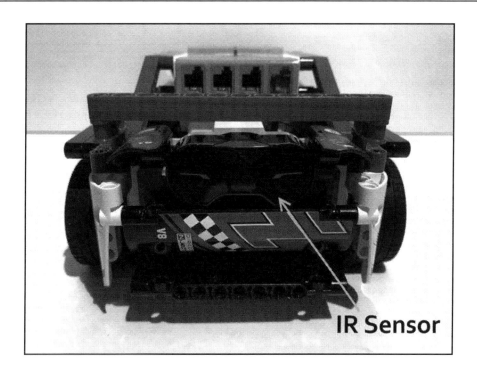

IR Sensor

Rotation sensor

This second sensor is not an external sensor like the IR sensor. Rather, it is located inside the EV3 motor. The Falcon makes extensive use of the rotation sensor (also referred to as an encoder) built into the medium motor that is used for steering (port A). The encoder provides information about the motor's current position in degrees, which the Falcon's program uses to coordinate the steering and facilitate its return-to-center feature. In short, the built-in encoder provides the steering with enough intelligence and makes the Falcon easier to drive.

Programming

Although the Falcon is remotely controlled by the user via a remote control, its RC program is quite intelligent because it coordinates the complex actions and decision making behind the scenes, resulting in a smooth and user-friendly program.

Control scheme

We should establish what each of the buttons on the EV3 remote will do. Earlier, we said that the driving and steering functions are independent of one another. We will program the controls accordingly: the left (red) side of the controller will control the driving, where up is forward and down is reverse; the right (blue) side will control the steering, where the up button will steer the Falcon's wheels to the right and the down button will steer them left:

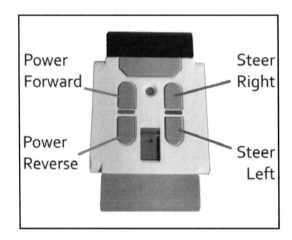

MyBlocks

The EV3 programming environment has a useful feature called the MyBlock editor. It allows you to save a chunk of EV3 code as a single block, so that you can use that sequence of code multiple times in a program or in other programs without having to rewrite it. Creating a MyBlock in EV3-G is analogous to defining a function in a text-based programming language.

We will create four MyBlocks for the Falcon's program; each executes a different aspect of the car steering. We use MyBlocks because these are fairly complex sequences of code and they appear multiple times throughout the RC program. Most of the Falcon's programming will be contained within these four MyBlocks. Creating MyBlocks for these important functions saves time and reduces the risk of making errors because we will only have to write each one once, and also makes the finished program easier to read.

Centering the steering

The first MyBlock we will make runs once at the very beginning of the program. It centers the Falcon's steering mechanism so that driving is easier for the user. It also resets the rotation sensor after it centers the wheels, which is important because it defines the center as the zero position, from which all of the later steering commands will be based.

Start programming just as you normally would; we do not have to worry about making the MyBlock until we are finished with the chunk of code that we want to save.

To start programming the steering centering MyBlock, drag out a loop block and set its exit case to **Motor Rotation** | **Compare** | **Current Power**. Set the threshold to **<** | 20 and make sure port A is selected. Within the loop, place a medium motor block (**On**, 25 percent power) and a `wait` block set to wait for 0.2 seconds.

This section of code turns the steering motor slowly in the positive direction. The loop block uses the built-in rotation sensor to check for a motor stall. The motor starts out at 25% power and, if the power drops below 20%, the program knows that the motor has stalled. The `short` wait block ensures that the motor has a chance to start moving and reach the target speed before the program starts looking for a motor stall:

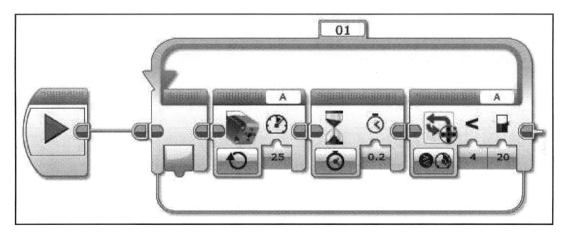

After that, place a medium motor block (**On for Degrees**, -75 percent power, 105 degrees, port A) followed by a motor rotation block (**Reset**, port A). The completed centering code looks like this:

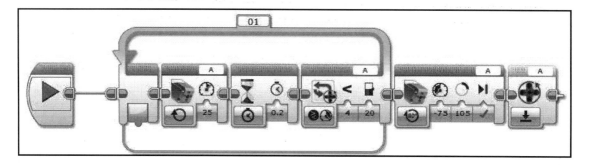

What is going on here? This code works by turning the steering mechanism in one direction until it cannot turn any more. At this point, the stall is detected, and the program rotates the motor back in the opposite direction for 105 degrees—the amount of rotation necessary to bring the steering back to the center position. Finally, it resets the rotation sensor on motor A, making the center position the new zero position. This is a convenient method because the program will automatically bring the wheels into the center position no matter what position they started in. This block makes the program more precise and user-friendly.

Saving code as a MyBlock

The chunk of code we made is the first of the four intelligent MyBlocks that make the Falcon's programming smart. Now that we have the code written out, follow these steps to save it as a MyBlock:

1. Click and drag your cursor to select all of the code that you wish to include in the MyBlock. The code that is successfully selected will be highlighted in blue. Do not include the Start block in your selection.
2. In the top-right corner of the screen, navigate to **Tools | My Block Builder**.
3. Using the **My Block Builder** wizard, set up your new MyBlock by naming it and selecting an icon. There are many icons to choose from, so choose an icon that represents what your new MyBlock does.
4. When you are satisfied, click **Finish** in the bottom-right corner of the wizard:

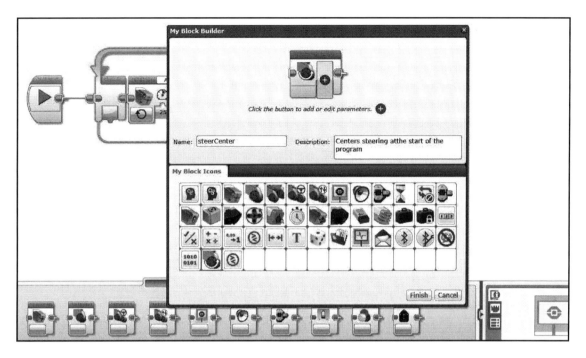

The MyBlock that we are making now should be called `steerCenter`. The MyBlock wizard also allows you to set up parameters; these are input and output values for your MyBlock. Since none of the MyBlocks we will make for the Falcon use parameters, you can ignore this for now, but it may prove to be useful in your later projects. We will extensively use the parameter feature in the next chapter.

After you click **Finish**, your code looks like this:

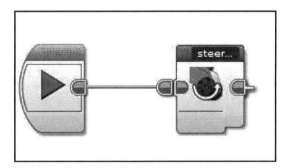

Congratulations! You have successfully saved your first MyBlock. The EV3 will execute all of the code contained within this MyBlock wherever you have placed it in the program. The MyBlock acts as a placeholder for all of the code we just wrote. If you need to edit a MyBlock, double click on it and it will expand to show all of the code contained inside.

All of the MyBlocks that you save will be stored under the teal programming tab at the bottom of the screen. You may now drag out your new MyBlock to use it anywhere in your program:

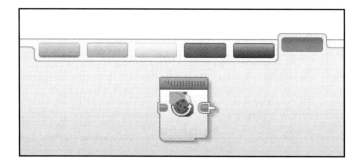

Steering left

The next MyBlock is fairly straightforward. It rotates the front wheels into the left position so that the Falcon will make a left turn.

Before the robot does anything, it needs to check the current position of the front wheels. Since cases in the full program can execute continuously for periods of time (for example, holding down the steering button on the remote to make a turn), the program needs to verify that the front wheels are not already in the left position. This makes sure that, after the wheels move into the left position, they stop and stay there. Otherwise, the steering will continue to turn left until it runs into a mechanical limit and locks up.

First, add a motor rotation block (**Measure** | **Degrees**, port A) and plug its output into the first input of a compare block. Set the compare state to less than (<) and change the comparison value (second input) to 45. Take the result from the compare block and plug it into the input of a switch set to logic. The switch is set to tabbed view to save space:

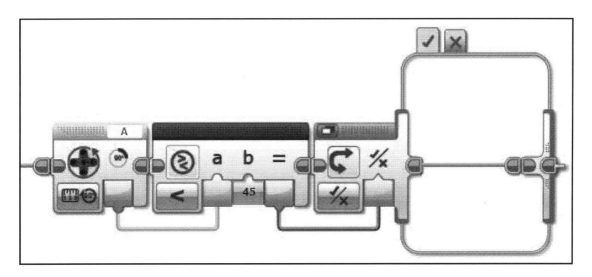

The *true* case of the switch executes if the degree value on the steering motor is less than 45, meaning the steering is not yet in the left position. Within the *true* case of the switch, we will add some code to move the wheels into the left position. Add a loop and set its exit case to **Motor Rotation** | **Compare** | **Degrees**. Set the threshold value to greater than or equal to (>=) 45 degrees and ensure that port A is selected. Within the loop, simply place a medium motor block (**On**, 100 percent power, port A):

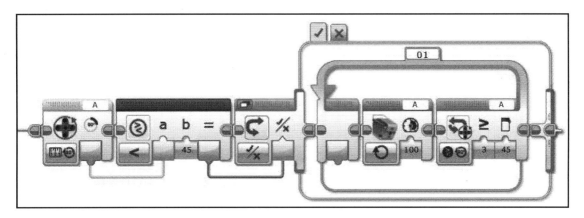

The number 45 means that the steering motor turns 45 degrees from center to make the Falcon's front wheels rotate. This value is adjustable. Increasing this value would cause the Falcon to make sharper turns, while decreasing it would cause it to make smoother turns. Experiment with different values to see what you like best. When you change the values, make sure that you change it in both of the places that it appears in the MyBlock, as well as both the left and right MyBlocks.

The *false* case of the switch executes when the degree value of motor A is equal to 45 degrees, which would indicate that the wheels are already in the left position, so no further action is required. Simply place a medium motor block that turns motor A **Off:**

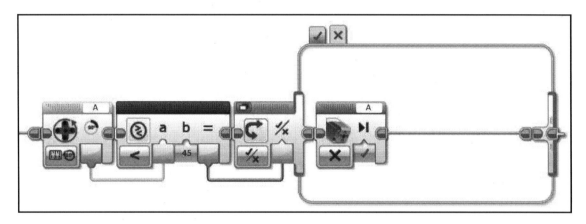

This is the completed code for the `steerleft` MyBlock. Save it using the MyBlock wizard following the steps outlined before, and name it `steerLeft`:

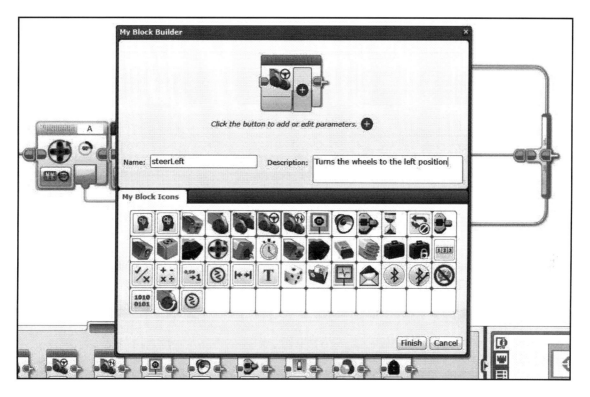

Steering right

Since we just completed the code for the `steerLeft` MyBlock, writing the code for the MyBlock that will steer the Falcon to the right will be easy because the programming is largely the same. You can make the `steerRight` MyBlock by following the same steps you used to make the `steerLeft` MyBlock. The only difference is that where the motor powers and threshold values were positive, they must now become negative and all of the inequality signs must be flipped:

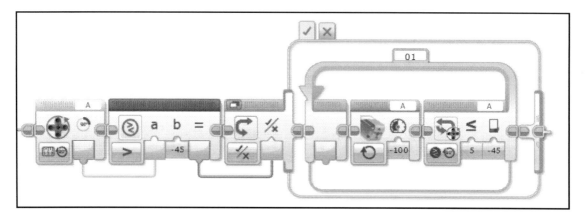

Do not forget to add a medium motor block to shut motor A off in the *false* case of the switch:

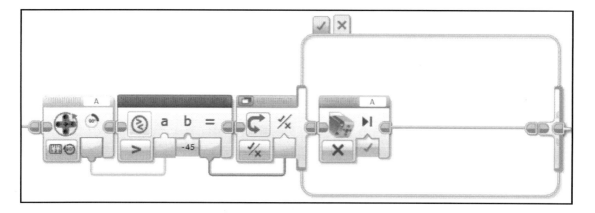

Finally, save the MyBlock as `steerRight` using the MyBlock builder.

Returning the steering to center

The final MyBlock is crucial to the car steering program. This MyBlock returns the steering mechanism to the center position regardless of what position it is currently in. This automatic return-to-center is a signature feature of the Falcon's programming.

This MyBlock starts by checking the position of the steering motor A. To be more specific, it actually first checks to see if the motor is in the left position; if this check returns *false*, then it checks to see if the motor is in the right position. If this returns *false* too, then the steering is already centered and no action is necessary.

The MyBlock first checks to see if the wheels are turned to the left (positive direction) by testing whether or not the degree value on motor A is greater than positive three (+3) degrees. The programming for this check looks like this:

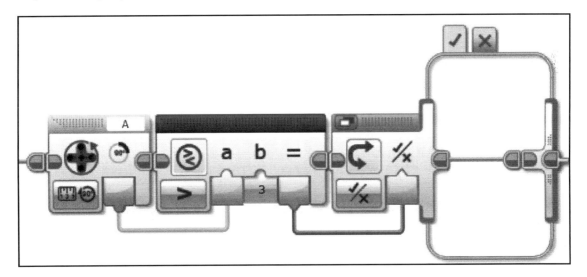

Setting the comparison value to 3 sets up a tolerance in the program, meaning that the MyBlock is satisfied when it brings the steering motor within three degrees in either direction of the center. You may wish to experiment with different tolerance levels; a smaller value would increase the precision of the steering, but could make it too sensitive. If you decide to change the tolerance, make sure that you change this value everywhere it appears.

If this check returns *true*, the wheels are currently steered left (positive direction), so the motor must rotate in the negative direction to bring the wheels back to the center. Within the true case of the switch, set up a loop (**Motor Rotation** | **Compare** | **Degrees**, < | 3, port A) and a medium motor block (**On**, -50 percent power, port A) such that it turns the steering motor to the right until it is within three degrees of the center:

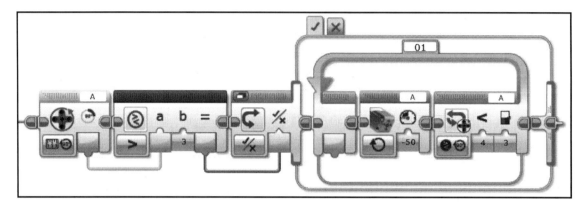

If the *false* case of the switch executes, then the steering is not in the left position. The program will now use a similar procedure to check if the steering is in the right position. It measures the degree position using the motor encoder, checks to see if it is less than -3 degrees, and executes the corresponding case of a logic switch:

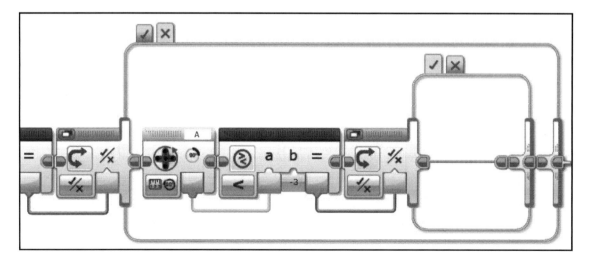

If this check returns *true*, then the wheels are currently steered right (negative direction), and the steering motor must turn in the positive direction to bring the wheels back to the center. Set up the loop (**Motor Rotation** | **Compare** | **Degrees**, > | –3, port A) and the medium motor block (**On**, 50 percent power, port A) in a similar manner to the way you set them up before. Since everything is in the opposite direction, you must negate all number values and flip the inequality sign:

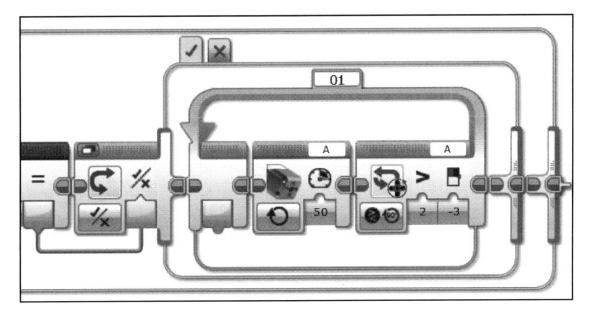

If this second switch returns *false*, then the steering is in the center and does not need to be adjusted. Simply shut the motor **Off**:

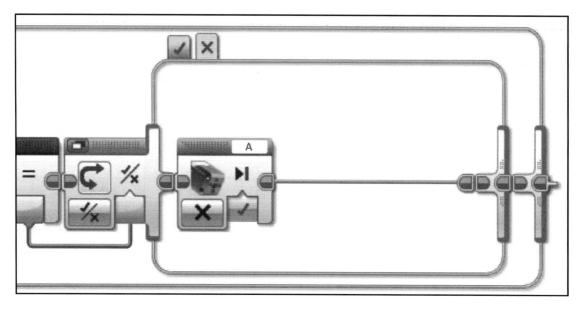

Finally, use the MyBlock Builder to save this section of code as a MyBlock called `steerReCenter`.

Assembling the program

We have finished making all of the MyBlocks; the bulk of the program is complete. Now, we can drop these blocks into the full program to make a fully-functional RC car.

Accessing your MyBlocks

The four MyBlocks that we have created can be found in your programming palate under the teal tab. They are ready to be added into your program wherever you need them:

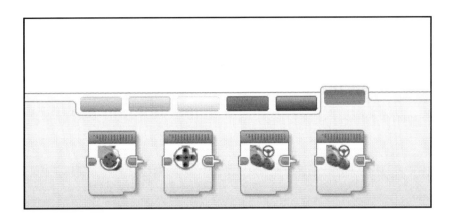

Getting started

Open up a new, blank program within your current project. This is where we will put the MyBlocks together to make the full RC program.

Start by adding your `steerCenter` MyBlock at the immediate start of the program. Centering and resetting the steering is the first thing the Falcon will do when the program starts. The MyBlock will be followed by a loop that repeats indefinitely:

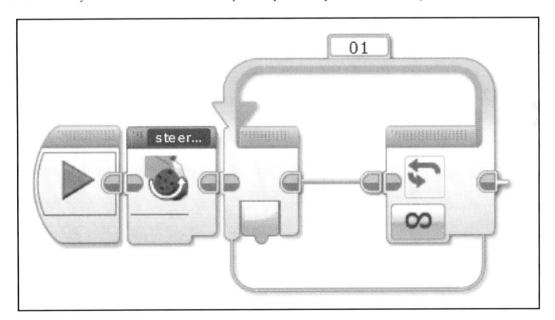

Place a switch within the loop. Change the switch's setting to **Infrared Sensor** | **Measure** | **Remote**, port 4, channel 1. Then, assign button ID **0** to the first case; select this as the default case by clicking on the circle on the button ID's tab (if this circle is not already filled). Assign button ID **1** to the second case. Press the **Add Case** button seven times to add additional cases:

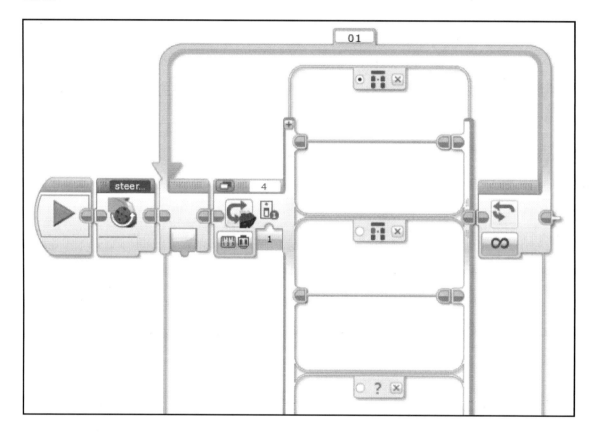

Programming the cases

The rest of the programming is straightforward, albeit monotonous. The difficult part of the programming is complete, but we still need to assign and program a case for every possible remote button combination (at least, the combinations we plan to use).

In the first case, no buttons are pressed (button ID **0**), so the Falcon should halt and center its steering. Recall that this is the default case, so the Falcon's preferred action is to idle if no remote buttons are pressed. Add the `steerReCenter` MyBlock and a move steering block (**Off**, ports B and C):

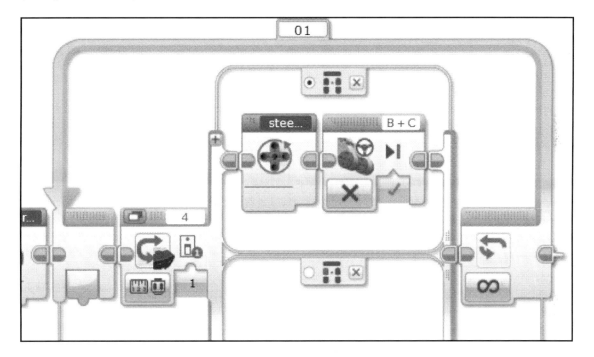

In the second case (button ID **1**), the robot is driving forward in a straight line. Add the `steerReCenter` MyBlock and a move steering block (**On**, Steering: 0, 100 percent power, port B and C):

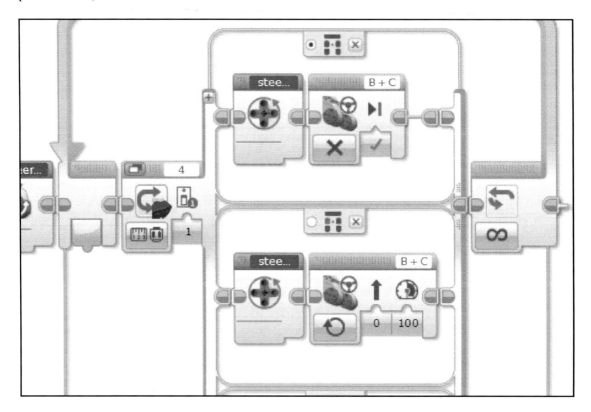

The two EV3 large motors in ports B and C must always move in the same direction with the same speed. We use a move steering block because it only has one power input, which speeds up the programming because we only need to enter one power value. Make sure that the steering value is always zero for this project; this will ensure that both drive motors turn in unison.

In the next case (button ID **2**), the Falcon drives in a straight line in reverse. Add `steerReCenter` and a move steering block set to −100 percent power:

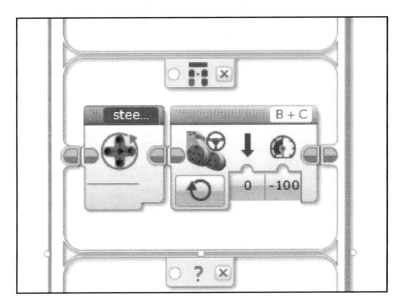

If the top-right button is pressed (button ID **3**), the Falcon's wheels will steer right without driving. Insert a `steerRight` MyBlock and a move steering block set to **Off:**

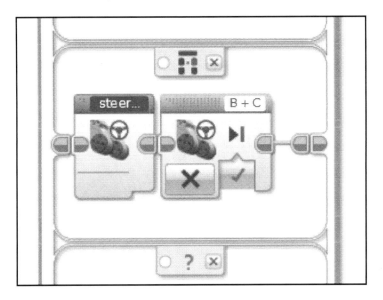

Similarly, if only the bottom-right button is pressed (button ID **4**), then the Falcon will steer its front wheels to the left without driving. Add the `steerLeft` block before a move steering block that shuts the drive motors off:

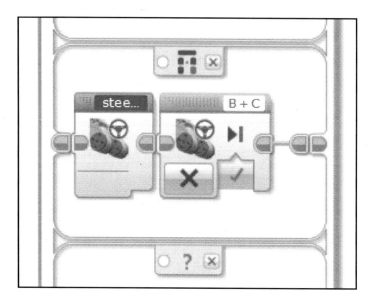

 Note that the `steerRight` and `steerLeft` MyBlocks use the same icon, and the full name is not displayed on the block. This can get confusing quickly. To avoid confusion, pay close attention to the name of the MyBlock you are placing. Hovering your cursor over the MyBlock will display its name. You may also choose different icons for the MyBlocks to further clarify the difference.

Now, we need to program the four double button cases. The first executes when both top buttons are pressed (button ID **5**) and causes the Falcon to steer right while driving forward. Place a `steerRight` block and a move steering block set to `100` percent power:

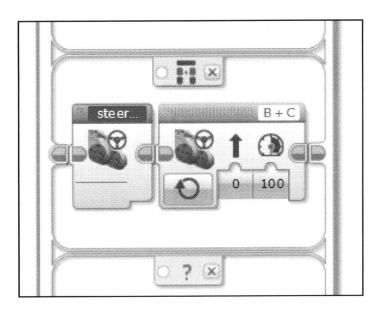

The second double button case executes when the top-left and bottom-right buttons are pressed in conjunction (button ID **6**). This makes the Falcon turn left while driving forward. Add the `steerLeft` block and a move steering block set to `100` percent power:

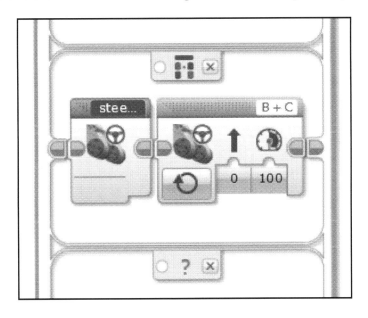

The penultimate case activates when the bottom-left and top-right buttons are pressed together (button ID 7). When this happens, the Falcon will steer right while driving in reverse. Add a `steerRight` block and a move steering block set to -100 percent power:

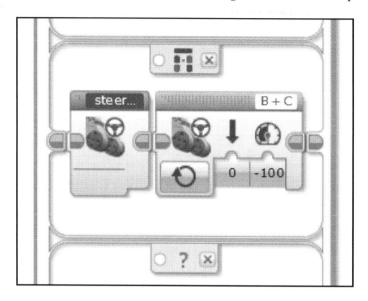

Finally, when both bottom buttons are pressed (button ID 8), the Falcon will steer left while driving in reverse. Insert a `steerLeft` MyBlock and a move steering block set to -100 percent power:

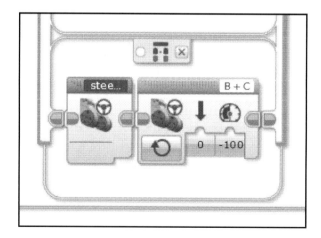

Putting it all together

The completed program looks like this:

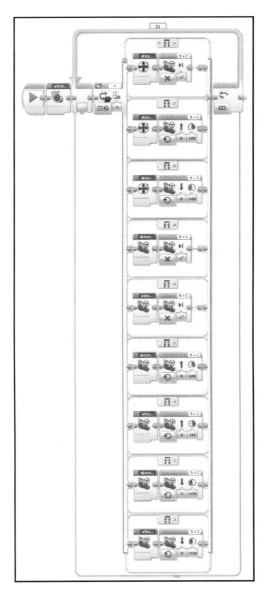

It looks fairly simple, right? That is because the most complex parts of the program are contained within the MyBlocks. Here, you can see that the MyBlocks make the program more readable. All of the smart programming used to control the steering resides within these MyBlocks.

Awesome! You now have a fully functional remote control race car!

Summary

In this chapter, we took our project in a completely new direction and broke away from tank-style driving to make a purpose-built speed machine. While building the Falcon, we learned about some of the mechanical components used to make a car-style drivetrain, such as the differential. We reapplied the rack-and-pinion mechanism to use it for steering. We discussed how each of the mechanical features in the Falcon relates to the design of cars in the real world.

We extensively used the rotation sensor built into the EV3 motors to coordinate an intelligent steering system. We also learned how to make MyBlocks and saw the advantages they bring when they are used in a program. We applied knowledge acquired in previous chapters to make a car-style remote control program. Finally, we resolved the paradox of a smart remote control car: even though the user controls the Falcon, its programming automatically coordinates a lot of complex decisions and actions behind the scenes.

In the next chapter, we will ditch the remote control altogether and program the Falcon to use a GPS receiver and a compass to navigate autonomously.

GPS Car – Autonomous EV3 Navigation

7

We are ready to make our final smart robot, the GPS Car! This smart vehicle is equipped with a GPS receiver and a digital magnetic compass, and its smart software allows the car to navigate to a pair of coordinates defined by the user. Yes, you can choose a location and the GPS Car will drive there! The GPS Car boasts sophisticated navigation sensors and advanced programming, which makes it the smartest robot in this book.

The GPS Car is based on the Falcon race car that we built in the previous chapter. We will convert the Falcon from remote control to autonomous by adding the navigation sensors and writing two new programs. The hardware will remain largely the same, which allows us to focus on writing our most sophisticated programs yet.

In this chapter, we will start by making some minor physical modifications to the Falcon and adding the new sensors. We will also cover some of the basic knowledge required to use the GPS and compass. Then, we will transition into the software and discuss how to prepare the EV3 in order to use third-party hardware. Finally, we will write two programs: the first is a simple GPS test program, which will help us get accustomed to using the GPS before we write the second program, an autonomous navigation program.

This project is especially relevant in the present day as many companies are currently prototyping autonomous cars for everyday use. The GPS Car that we will make in this chapter is far simpler, but it uses some navigation concepts that are employed in real-world autonomous cars. Therefore, this project is a stepping stone to understanding the technology used by full-scale self-driving cars.

This is the first (and only) project in this book that requires non-LEGO elements. The GPS receiver and compass are manufactured for use with the EV3 by third-party manufacturers Dexter Industries and HiTechnic, respectively. We will learn more about these sensors in the following sections.

The time is ripe for us to dive in and make our smartest robot yet:

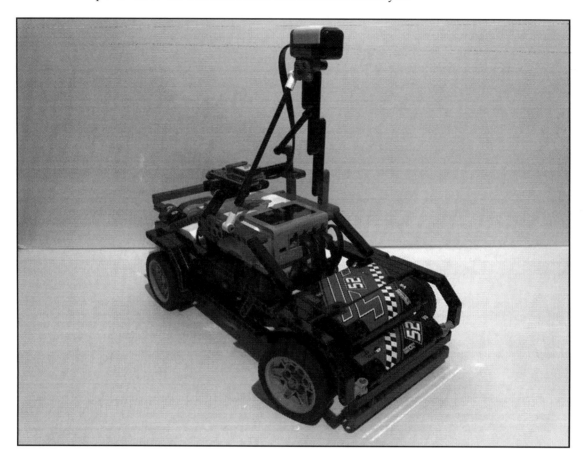

Technical requirements

You must have EV3 Home Edition Software V1.2.2 or newer installed on your computer. You may also install LEGO Digital Designer (LDD) V4.3 and download the LDD file for this project to guide you in the building process.

The LDD file is available on the **Downloads** page of the Builderdude35 website:

http://builderdude35.com/download/gps-car-ldd/

The LDD and EV3 files for this chapter are available on GitHub:

`https://github.com/PacktPublishing/Building-Smart-LEGO-MINDSTORMS-EV3-Robots/tree/master/Chapter07`

Check out this video to see the robot in action:

`https://goo.gl/gCAZQ9`

Hardware

We will use the Falcon as the base robot and do some modifications that will enable it to navigate autonomously. Make sure that you have read the previous chapter and that you are familiar with how the Falcon's hardware works before you proceed.

We will be adding two navigation sensors to the Falcon: a Dexter Industries dGPS and a HiTechnic compass sensor. We will take a look at how each of these sensors works and how they will enable the Falcon to navigate autonomously:

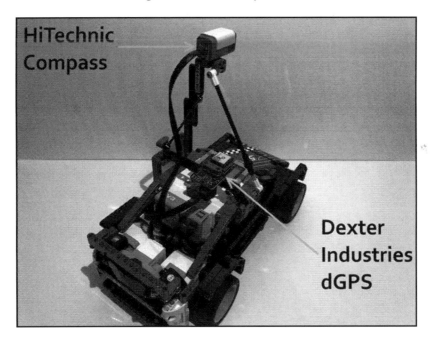

Dexter Industries dGPS

This is a simple GPS chip that connects to the satellites that orbit the Earth to give us an estimate of where the EV3 is in the world. The dGPS provides information such as UTC (time), latitude, longitude, heading, velocity, and satellite link status. We will only need the first three when we write the programs for this project.

On one side of the board is the GPS antenna and the signal LED. The other side is where the battery and sensor plug are mounted. When mounting the dGPS on a robot, the antenna should face up so that it has a clearer view of the sky. We will discuss mounting the sensor in more detail shortly. Here, the dGPS is shown with the battery side facing up (plus some extra Technic pins used for mounting, which we will discuss soon):

Basic principles of GPS navigation

In order to use the dGPS, it is imperative that we understand the basics of GPS navigation.

The two components of a GPS coordinate are latitude and longitude. Together, these two numbers allow a GPS receiver to pinpoint its exact position on Earth. Mapping systems such as Google Maps use a decimal-degree format to represent latitude and longitude, meaning these values are in the form `dd.mmmmmm`. The dGPS provides latitude and longitude information in an integer decimal-degree format, which means it always expresses position figures as an integer, or whole number, in the form `ddmmmmmm`. You can think of it as a decimal-degree format where the decimal point has been removed. For example, a hypothetical latitude value in decimal-degree format could be `40.948162` degrees; the dGPS would report this latitude as `40948162`.

The sign of the latitude and longitude values indicate which hemisphere the GPS receiver is located in. A positive latitude indicates that the GPS is in the northern hemisphere, and a negative latitude indicates a location in the southern hemisphere; the greater the magnitude of the latitude value, the farther the GPS is from the equator. A positive longitude value indicates that the GPS is in the eastern hemisphere, and a negative longitude indicates a location in the western hemisphere; the magnitude of the longitude value indicates the distance from the prime meridian.

In an open field, a GPS receiver can pinpoint its location to within 1–3 meters. Environmental obstructions such as trees or buildings block the GPS receiver's line of sight to the sky and cause the signal sent by the satellite to bounce before it reaches the GPS receiver. This causes the GPS's accuracy to decrease. To obtain the best accuracy, use the dGPS in an environment with few obstructions. Because there is always some amount of error inherent in determining GPS position, the coordinates provided by a GPS receiver are considered estimates.

Using the dGPS

The dGPS has an LED that lights up in a solid color when it has connected to four satellites, the minimum number of connections required to estimate a position. The dGPS will only provide new position information while it has a satellite connection. If the connection is lost, the LED will turn off.

When powering the EV3 brick on, the LED on the dGPS will flash to indicate that it is receiving power and has started looking for satellites to connect to. The time it takes for the dGPS to acquire a connection with four satellites varies depending on the environment the dGPS is in. Nearby trees and buildings block the dGPS's line of sight and increase the time it takes to acquire a satellite link.

When the dGPS is powered on for the first time, it can take up to ten minutes for it to acquire its first satellite signal. This is because the dGPS needs to create an almanac of all of the available satellite connections. Signal acquisition will be faster for each successive startup.

While there is a valid satellite link, the dGPS will update with new position information once every second. When writing a program that includes the dGPS, a 1-second wait should be programmed after each time the EV3 reads data from the sensor.

HiTechnic compass

This sensor is a digital magnetic compass that measures the Earth's magnetic field to find the position of the Earth's magnetic poles. This sensor outputs a value from 0 to 359 degrees, which indicates the sensor's current absolute heading (the angle that the sensor faces) based off of magnetic north. A heading value of 0 degrees means that the sensor is facing due north; 90 degrees indicates that the sensor is facing east, 180 degrees is south, and 270 degrees is west:

The sensor also has a relative heading feature, which allows the user to set a target heading. The target heading becomes the new zero position. Relative heading values range from −179 to +180 degrees; a positive relative heading value indicates that the robot must turn right (clockwise) to reach the target direction, and a negative relative heading value means that the robot must turn left (counterclockwise). A relative heading value of zero indicates that the robot is perfectly on track with the target and does not need to adjust its trajectory. The GPS Car will rely on the relative heading feature in its navigation program.

Using the compass

Although the compass is simpler to use than the dGPS, there is still one important rule to follow when incorporating the compass into an EV3 robot. The compass is designed to measure the Earth's magnetic field, but the electronic and metal components in a robot can create their own local magnetic fields or distort the field that the compass is trying to measure. To minimize interference, the compass should be mounted on the robot so that it is at least ten centimeters away from the robot's EV3 brick, motors, batteries, or other sensors. In the following section, we will describe a specific mount for the GPS Car.

 For more information about these sensors, visit their respective manufacturers' websites. The dGPS is manufactured by Dexter Industries, and the compass is manufactured by HiTechnic.

Modifying the Falcon

Now, we will make a few changes to the Falcon to accommodate these new sensors.

Add a Technic beam that runs the width of the vehicle and sits a few centimeters above the EV3 brick. Mount the dGPS on this beam and ensure that the antenna side of the chip faces skyward. The best way to mount the dGPS to Technic elements is using a Technic crossblock and two of the blue cross-to-friction pegs, as shown in the following image; this method ensures that the dGPS is securely mounted and minimizes mechanical stress on the fragile GPS board. You may choose to place it slightly off-center so that it does not obstruct access to the EV3 brick. Plug the dGPS into sensor port 1:

Next, build a long stalk on one side of the robot that reaches at least ten centimeters above the EV3 brick; this is where we will mount the compass. Placing the compass atop a tall tower increases the distance between it and other electronic components, which minimizes the electromagnetic interference that the other electronics will impart on the compass. Finally, reinforce the compass tower with some Technic axles and rods so that the tower will not wobble under the compass's weight. Plug the compass into port 2:

With these modifications completed, we are ready to start working on the GPS Car's software.

Software

We will write two programs for the GPS Car. The first program is a simple GPS test program, and the second is the autonomous navigation program. Before we start programming, we will need to prepare the EV3 software for use with the third-party hardware.

Preparing the EV3 software

The dGPS and compass require specific software for them to be used with the EV3. Both sensors have their own programming block, which allows you to program the third-party sensor like you would program a standard EV3 sensor. Thankfully, the software is available for download for free from the manufacturers' websites. All we need to do is follow a few steps to download the third-party software and import it into the EV3 programming environment.

The steps for installing the Dexter Industries and HiTechnic software are the same, so we will start with the Dexter Industries software. All of Dexter Industries' software is available on their GitHub repositories. We will need the software from their EV3 repository, which you can access here: `https://github.com/DexterInd/EV3_Dexter_Industries_Sensors`.

After you have found the repository, follow these steps to import the Dexter Industries software into your EV3 programming environment:

1. Download the Dexter Industries repository from GitHub. After the download finishes, extract the files and save them to a destination on your computer.
2. Start the EV3 software and open to a new project. Navigate to the toolbar and select **Tools | Block Import and Export Wizard**.
3. Click the **Browse** button in the wizard. Navigate to the destination where you saved the software you extracted earlier. Open the folder containing the Dexter Industries firmware; select the file named `Dexter.ev3b` and click **OK**.
4. The **Block Import and Export** wizard will now show that the `Dexter.ev3b` file is selected and is ready to be imported. Click the **Import** button at the bottom-right corner of the wizard:

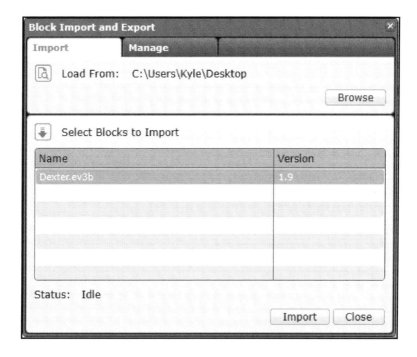

5. You will receive a message that indicates whether the import was completed successfully. If so, then the final step is to restart the EV3 software so the changes can take effect. The next time you start the software and open a project, the Dexter Industries blocks will appear in the sensor block palate.

The programming blocks for all of the Dexter Industries blocks are included in the file that we imported. We will only need the dGPS block, so you can ignore the rest of the blocks for this project.

We will follow the same steps to import the HiTechnic programming blocks into the EV3 software. The download can be found at `http://www.hitechnic.com/file.php?f=841-HiTechnicEV3Blocks.zip` and the name of the file we need to download is `841-HiTechnicEV3Blocks.zip`. Each of the HiTechnic sensor blocks is separate, so when you select the file to import in step 3, choose `HTCompass.ev3b` to import the software for the compass sensor.

After you finish importing the programming blocks, you sensor palate will expand to include the new third-party blocks you added. These blocks are ready for use, which means that we can start writing our programs.

GPS test program

We will now make a simple GPS test program. This will give us experience with using the dGPS before we write the complex navigation program. The test program reads the current time, latitude, and longitude from the dGPS and prints it to the EV3 display.

Sensor blocks

First, place three dGPS sensor blocks inside an infinite loop. Each dGPS block reads a different piece of information from the sensor. The first one reads the UTC time, the second one reads the current latitude, and the third one reads the current longitude. You can set the block to read the desired information by clicking on the bottom-left corner of the block and selecting the proper mode:

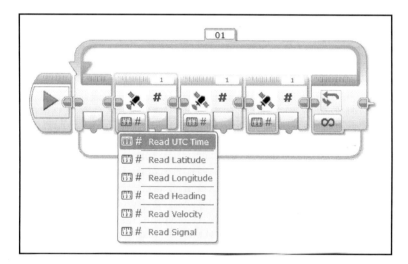

Text blocks

Next, place three text blocks after the sensor blocks; these are found under the red data operations tab in the programming palate:

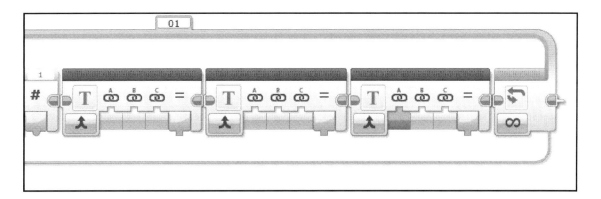

These blocks allow us to print the sensor data next to a static label on the EV3 screen. For example, in our program, we will print the word UTC: followed by the UTC value read from the dGPS on one line on the EV3 screen. Each of the three text blocks pairs with one of the dGPS sensor blocks to merge the sensor's value with the label so it can be printed to the EV3 screen.

We can now set up the labels. They correspond to the data being printed on the EV3 screen, so we will have one label that says UTC:, one that says Lat:, and one for Lon:. Type the labels into the first input of each text block. When finished, they look like this:

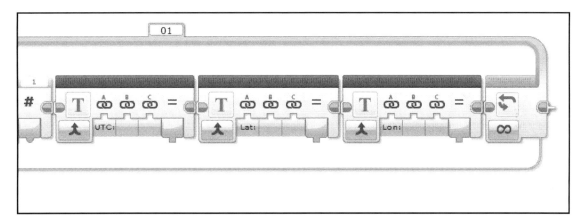

With the labels in place, we can start matching the sensor data to each text block. The first sensor block reads the UTC from the dGPS. Plug the data wire from this sensor block into the second input of the text block that you set up with the UTC: label:

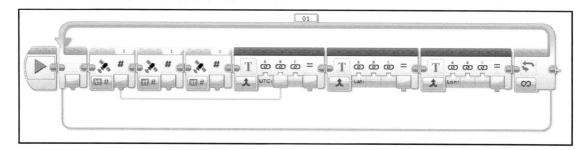

Repeat this process for the remaining two block pairs; the dGPS block that reads latitude should be paired to the text block with the Lat: label, and the block that reads longitude should be paired to the text block with the Lon: label.

When all of the sensor blocks and text blocks are correctly paired, the program looks like this:

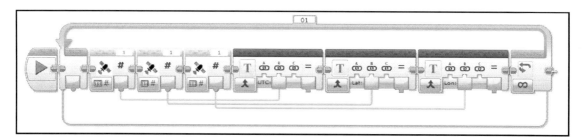

Display blocks

The next step is to add the display blocks that print the merged text to the EV3 screen. Start by placing a display block directly after the text blocks:

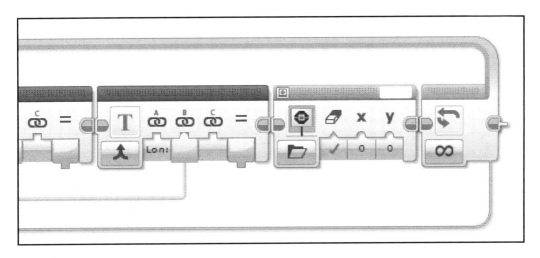

By default, the display block is set to print an image to the EV3 screen. Click on the bottom-left corner of the display block to change its mode to **Text** | **Grid**:

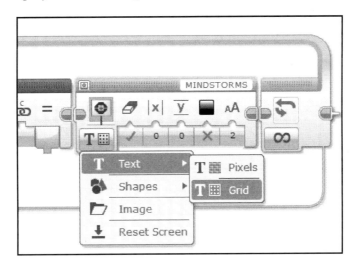

The block changes to reflect the new mode. However, there is still more setup to do. We must change the text that the block will print to the EV3 display. By default, the block will print the text typed into the top-right corner of the block. Click on the white space in the top-right corner of the block and select **Wired**. The block will change again, this time to include a data wire input. Now, the block will print the text it receives from the attached data wire:

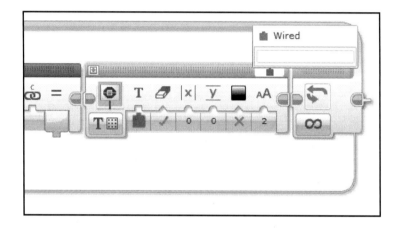

Add two more text blocks and follow the same steps to set them up:

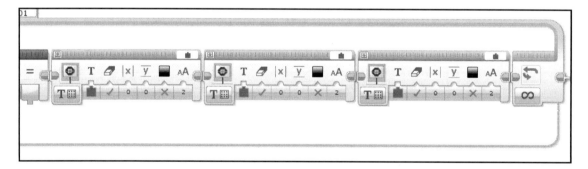

Now that all three display blocks are in place, we can set the font size and assign each string of text to a line on the EV3 display.

The last input on the display block controls the font size. Change this to 0, the smallest font size available, on all of the blocks.

We also need to assign each text block to a separate line so they do not overwrite each other. The fourth input of the display block assigns the text to a row on the EV3 screen. Set the first display block to print on line 1 (this is actually the second line, because the EV3 starts counting lines at zero). Assign the second block to line 3 and the third to line 5.

The final step in setting up the display blocks is very important, yet easily overlooked. The second input on the display block contains a true/false value that controls whether that block will erase the EV3 display before printing its text. This should be set to *true* for the first block, but *false* for the second and third blocks. This is so that each time the program loops around, it erases the old information from the EV3 display, but the second and third blocks do not erase the new information printed by the block before them.

When the setup for the display blocks is complete, they look like this:

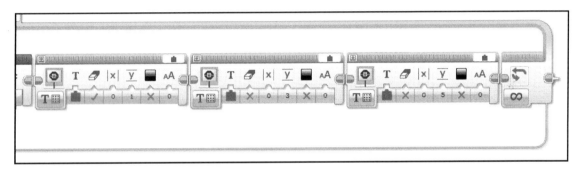

Now, take the data wire from each text block and plug it into the text input of one of the display blocks. UTC should go to the first display block, latitude should go to the second, and longitude should go to the third:

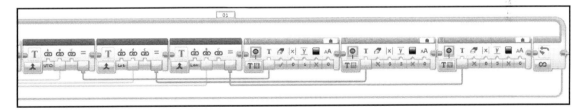

Wait block

Recall that the dGPS updates with new information once per second. To prevent the program from sampling the dGPS too quickly, add a wait block (set for one second) at the end:

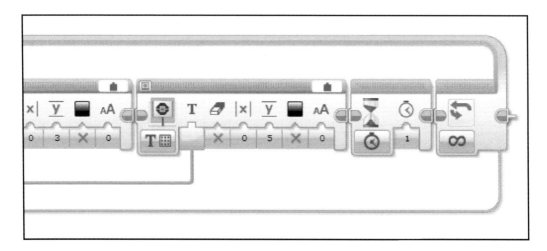

Putting it all together

The completed GPS test program looks like this:

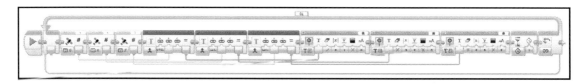

You can use this program to test your dGPS and gather some sample coordinates. We have also gained some experience with programming the dGPS, which will guide us through writing the navigation code.

Autonomous navigation

This program allows you to type in a pair of GPS coordinates and the car will use the dGPS and compass to drive there. The program is quite sophisticated compared to all of the programs we have made so far, so hang on!

Acquiring target coordinates

You may use the GPS test program to find some target GPS coordinates for the car to navigate to. You may also use Google Maps; click on a location on the map and that location's latitude and longitude will be displayed in decimal-degree format. For example, here are the coordinates for the **Washington Monument**:

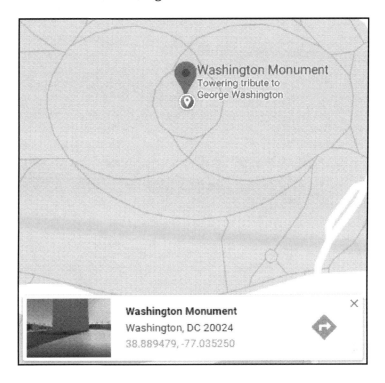

After you have acquired a pair of target coordinates, you may proceed with the programming.

MyBlocks for car steering

The navigation program relies on MyBlocks to do the bulk of the work. We will make five MyBlocks in total. We will start with the four car-steering MyBlocks because they are a review from the last chapter.

Importing/exporting MyBlocks

The first MyBlock we need is steerCenter; we created this MyBlock in the last chapter. Fortunately, we can use the EV3 software's MyBlock import/export feature to save some time and avoid rewriting the MyBlock. This tool allows you to export a MyBlock from one EV3 project to a destination on your computer, then import the MyBlock into another EV3 project. This will allow us to copy the MyBlocks we wrote for the Falcon and use them for the GPS Car.

Follow these steps to copy a MyBlock from one EV3 project file to use it in another project:

1. Open the project that contains the MyBlock you wish to reuse. For this chapter, we are copying the steerCenter MyBlock from the Falcon project, so open the Falcon's EV3 project file. Locate the **Project Properties** icon near the top left corner of the screen:

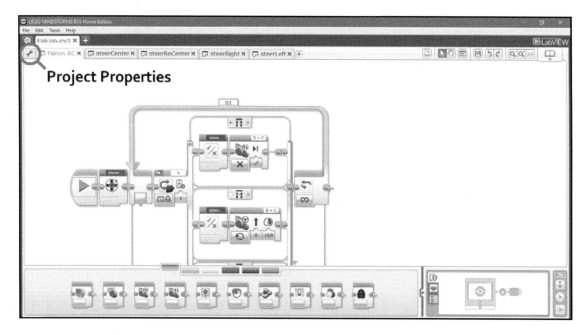

2. Click on the icon to open the **Project Properties** menu. This menu allows you to import and export programs, images, sounds, MyBlocks, and variables to and from the EV3 project file. Locate the **My Blocks** tab and click on it:

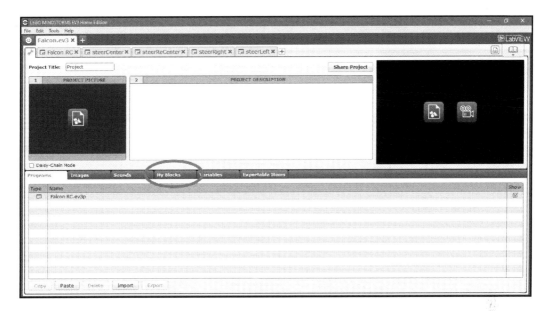

3. The menu displays the four MyBlocks that we created for the Falcon. Click on the desired MyBlock, steerCenter, to select it. Then, click the **Export** button near the bottom of the menu:

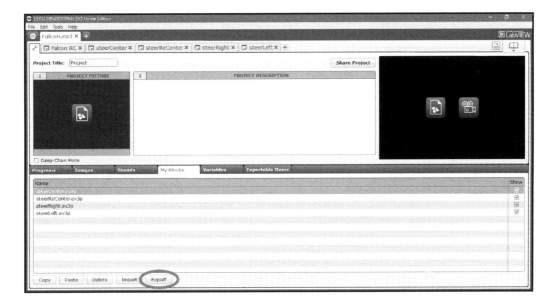

4. Name your MyBlock and save it to a destination on your computer:

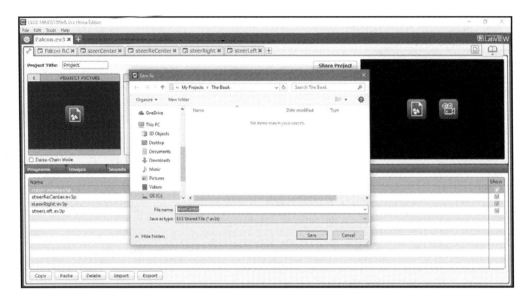

5. Now that the MyBlock has been exported from the Falcon project and saved on to the computer, we must import it into the GPS Car project. Open the GPS Car project, navigate to its **Project Properties** menu, click on the **My Blocks** tab, and click on the **Import** button near the bottom of the menu:

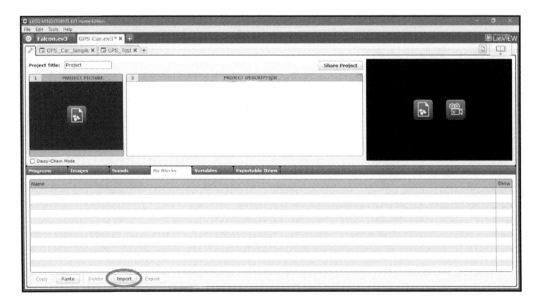

6. Open the destination your saved the MyBlock to earlier. Then, select and open the MyBlock:

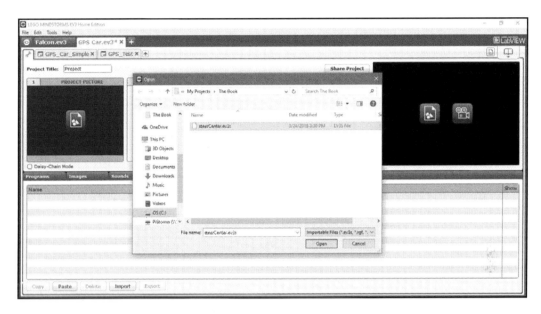

7. The new MyBlock is now displayed in the menu for the GPS Car project, indicating that it was successfully imported and is ready for use:

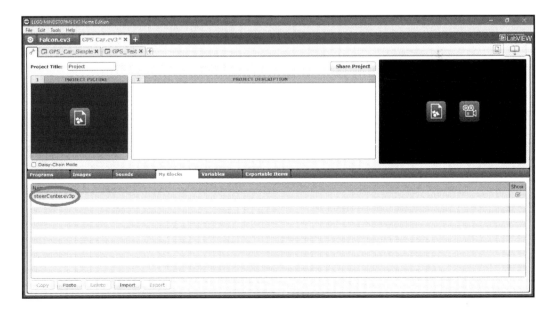

8. Exit the **Project Properties** menu by clicking on the tab of one of the project's programs. Just as if we had written the MyBlock directly into the project, the new MyBlock is now available in the programming palate:

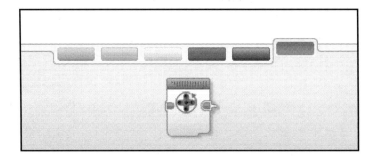

If you drag the newly imported MyBlock into a program and double click it, it will expand to show the code within. You can see that the import was successful because you can recognize the code from the previous chapter:

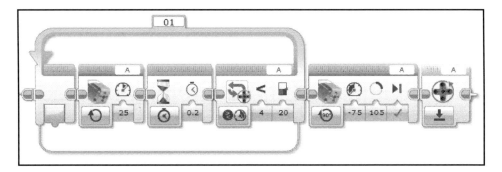

We will also directly borrow the steerRcCenter MyBlock from the Falcon project. Follow the preceding steps to import this block into the GPS Car project too:

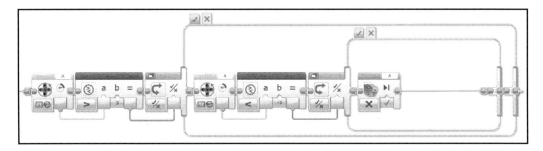

Steering left and right

We must also make MyBlocks for steering the wheels left and right. We cannot directly borrow these from the previous project; while the steering MyBlocks we made for the Falcon project are very precise, we cannot use them because the navigation program starts to become too complex for them to work. Instead, we will opt for a simpler alternative: a simple switch block that checks the current position of the steering motor. If the motor is less than 45 degrees from the center, the program rotates the motor 45 degrees. Here is the simplified steerLeft MyBlock:

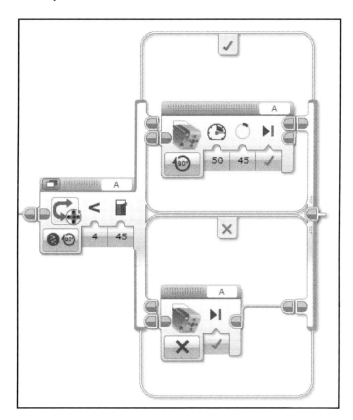

And here is the simple `steerRight` MyBlock, which is a mirror image of `steerLeft`:

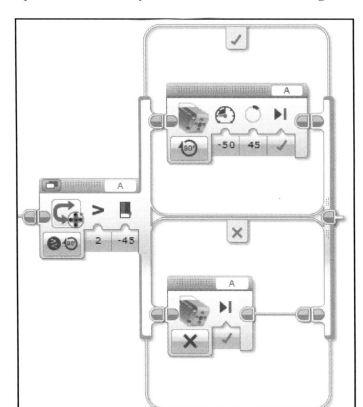

You can change the magnitude of the steering corrections by changing the target value from 45 degrees to your desired number of degrees.

Unfortunately, these steering MyBlocks are somewhat clumsy, but they will suffice. Because the program as a whole stretches the limits of the EV3 brick's capabilities, we need to use these simple steering blocks.

getAngle MyBlock

This is the fifth MyBlock used in the navigation program. With this MyBlock, you can plug in the current position (latitude/longitude) and the target position, and it will calculate the angle at which that the robot needs to drive to in order to reach the destination; in short, it tells the robot what direction to drive in. As we make this block, we will learn about variables and parameters. We will also incorporate some advanced math.

Program

To start, drag out a math block (set to subtract) and a variable block. Both are found under the red data operations tab of the programming palate:

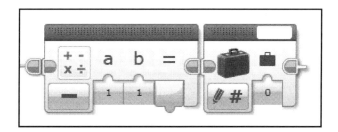

 A variable is a placeholder for a value. They have two operations: write, which changes the value stored in the variable, and read, which retrieves the stored value. This means that variables are a convenient way to save a value in one part of a program to use it in another part of the code. In the EV3 software, variables can store three types of data: numeric, logic, and text.

A variable must be defined before we can use it in the program. The first step is to choose the data type. By default, variables in the EV3 software are set to numeric. Luckily, that is what we need, so we do not have to change it. Next, we must give it a name. Click on the white space in the top-right corner of the block and select **Add Variable**. A window appears into which you can type the name of the new variable:

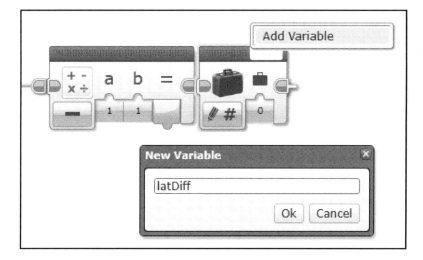

The name of this specific value is latDiff, which is shorthand for latitude difference. Our MyBlock calculates the difference between the destination latitude and the current latitude and stores it in this variable.

Now that the first variable is in place, we can continue with the programming. The data wire output from the first math block will get plugged into the input of latDiff, meaning that the result from the subtraction operation will be stored in that variable. That same data wire will get plugged into a compare block, which checks to see if the resulting value is equal to zero. The result from the compare block will control a switch (set to logic). In the *true* case of the switch, place another variable block with its mode set to **Write** | **Numeric** and choose latDiff again. Enter a value of 1 into the input of the block. Leave the *false* case of the switch empty. The start of the getAngle code looks like this:

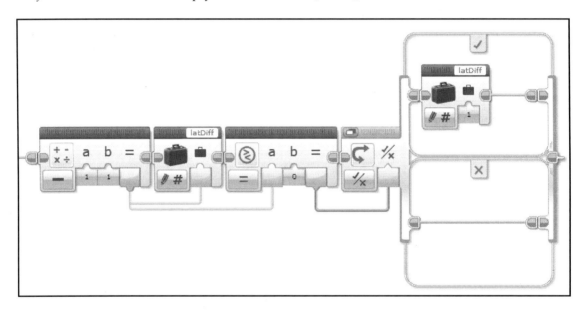

What is going on here? The segment of code that we just wrote will subtract the current latitude (read from the dGPS) from the destination latitude and store the difference in the latDiff variable. Then, the code checks to see if the difference equals zero. If so, then the program reassigns a value of 1 to the latDiff variable; this is a necessary step because latDiff will be the denominator of a division operation, and dividing by zero will cause an error.

You may also be wondering about the inputs of that subtraction block. We will revisit them later when we turn this code into a MyBlock because we will set up some parameters, which allow us to plug in the destination latitude and GPS latitude as inputs.

The program also needs to find the difference between the destination longitude and current longitude. Set up another subtraction math block that saves its result to a new variable called `longDiff`. We do not need the extra step that checks for a zero value because `longDiff` will be the numerator of the division operation. Again, ignore the input of the math block for now because we will define some parameters later:

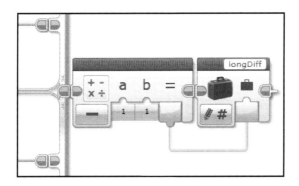

In the EV3 software, the dGPS reports all latitude and longitude values as positive numbers. This is problematic if the car is in the western or southern hemisphere; if this is the case, add another math block that multiplies the current GPS value by −1. The setup will look like this (we will discuss how to configure the parameters in this case later). Here is the modified code that adjusts longitude if the receiver is in the western hemisphere:

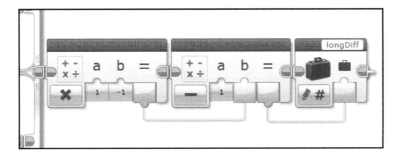

Now that `latDiff` and `longDiff` have been calculated and stored, we can use them in our program to calculate an angle. We will use some trigonometry concepts to calculate the angle. Imagine that `latDiff` and `longDiff` are the legs (the two shortest sides) of a right triangle. We can divide the difference in longitude by the difference in latitude and take the inverse tangent to calculate an angle in degrees.

Take out two variable blocks, one for `latDiff` and one for `longDiff`, but set them to **Read** | **Numeric** mode to retrieve the data stored in them. Then, add a math block and set it to **Advanced** mode:

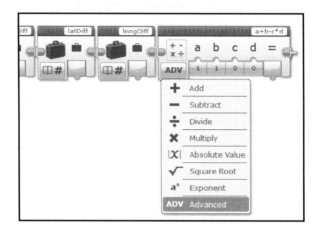

The advanced math block allows us to access more complex operations and perform multiple operations within one block. When you click on the white space in the top-right corner, you will be able to type in the desired operation. To calculate the angle, we will need to divide `longDiff` by `latDiff` and then take the inverse tangent. So, type in `atan(a/b)`. The variables `a` and `b` correspond to the math block's inputs (`c` and `d` will not be used in this project):

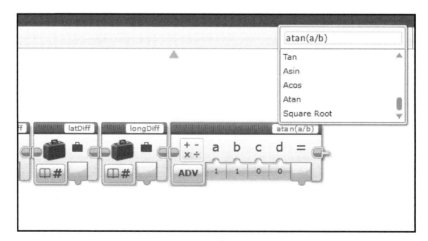

Insert the value of `longDiff` to the a input of the advanced math block, and assign `latDiff` to input b. Create a new numeric variable named `angle` into which the result of the advanced math block will be stored:

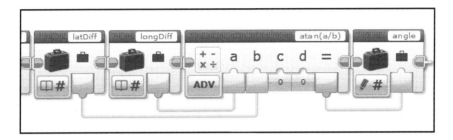

The code now calculates an angle, which can tell the car which way to turn. However, we are not finished yet. The sign of `latDiff` and `longDiff` indicate direction; however, a negative in either `latDiff` or `longDiff` will make the whole fraction negative and throw off the angle calculation. Additionally, if both `latDiff` and `longDiff` are negative, the math block will return the same angle value as if both were positive, despite the fact that negatives on both values indicates that the car must drive in the opposite direction! We need to add some cases that check the sign of `latDiff` and `longDiff` and make adjustments to the angle value we calculated.

First, check to see if the denominator is negative. Read `latDiff`, use a compare block to check if the value is less than zero, and use the result to control a logic switch:

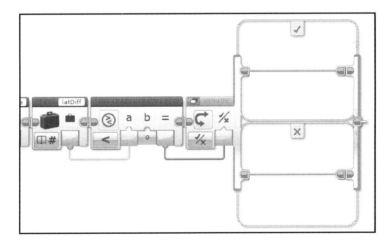

If this test returns *true*, also check `longDiff` for a negative value. In the *true* case of the switch you just placed, program some code that tests to see if the value of `longDiff` is less than zero; programming the code for this check is very similar to the one we just made:

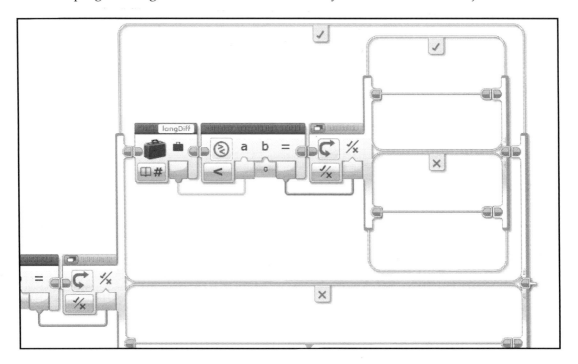

If both checks return *true*, then both the numerator (`longDiff`) and denominator (`latDiff`) are negative. We must subtract 180 degrees from the calculated angle value to compensate. In the *true* case of the second switch, program some code that reads the value stored in the angle variable, subtract 180, then write it to the angle variable again to save it as the new value:

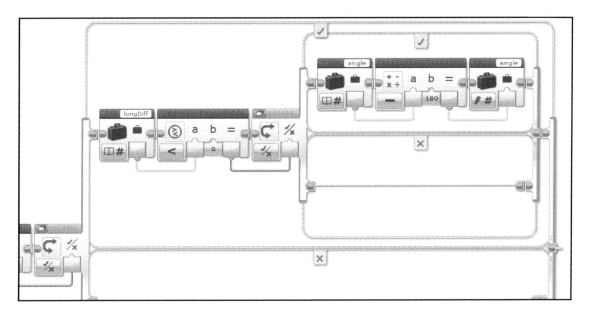

If the first check returns *true*, but the second check returns *false*, then only the denominator is negative. We will need to add 180 degrees to the value stored in the angle variable:

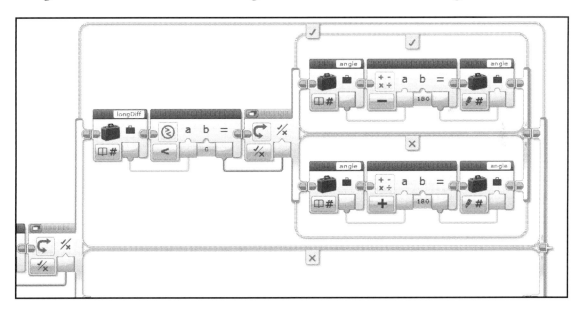

If the first check returns *false*, then the denominator is positive. However, we still need to check the sign of the numerator. Add another check that evaluates the sign of `longDiff`:

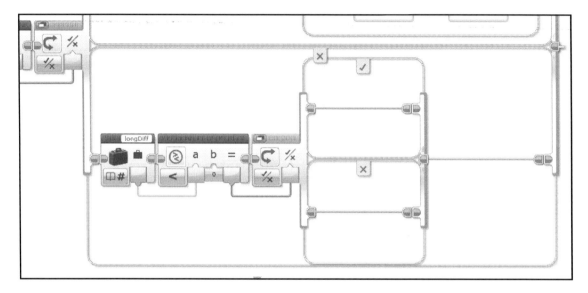

If the numerator is negative, then we will need to add 360 degrees to the angle value:

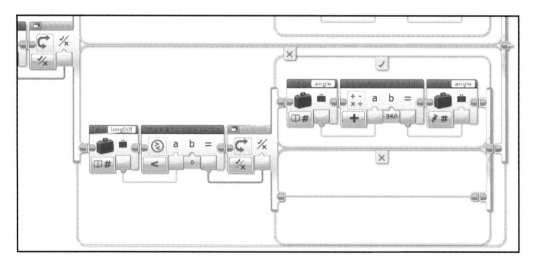

If both checks return *false*, then the numerator and denominator were both positive and no adjustment is necessary. Leave the final *false* case empty.

The final bit of code reads the angle value after the necessary adjustments have been made. It uses a round block to round the calculated angle to the nearest whole number. The result of the round block is the final angle output of the MyBlock. We will set up a parameter to capture this output soon:

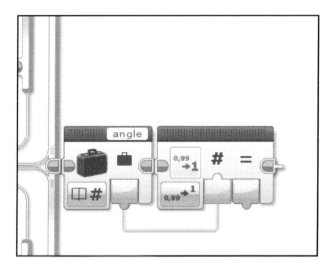

Here is the completed EV3 code for calculating the angle. We will now save the code in a MyBlock:

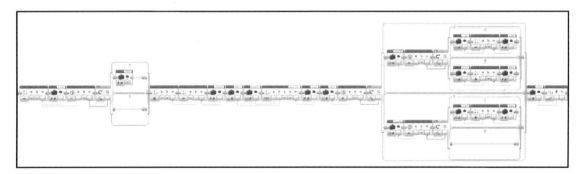

Save as MyBlock and create parameters

Select all of the code (excluding the start block), open the **My Block Builder**, and name the
MyBlock getAngle. Now, we will start setting up the parameters; click the button to create
a total of five parameters:

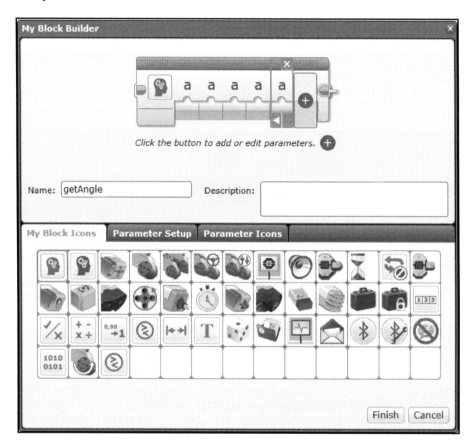

Click on the **Parameter Setup** tab to configure each parameter. By default, the parameters are set to a numeric input. The first four parameters of the getAngle block are numeric inputs, so we can leave them in their default settings. All we need to do for these first four is name them. The names of the four inputs in order are curLat (current latitude), curLong (current longitude), destLat (destination latitude), and destLong (destination longitude):

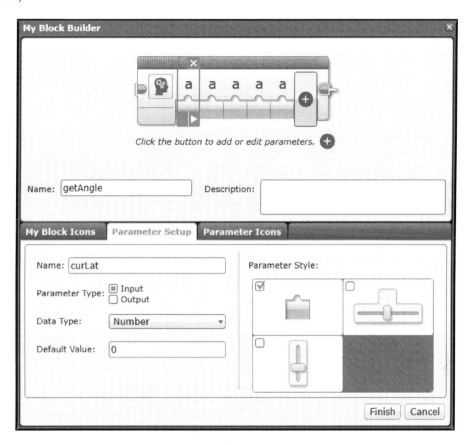

The final parameter is called `angle`, and it is the numeric output of the MyBlock. After naming it, make sure that **Output** and **Number** are selected:

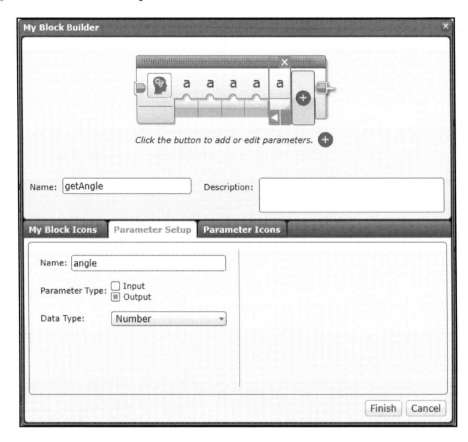

Then, click on the **Parameter Icons** tab. Here, you can select icons for each parameter. For example, you may choose to use letters **a** through **d** for the four numeric inputs and an angle icon for the output:

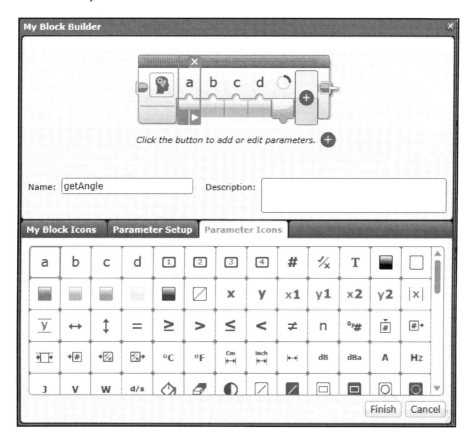

After you have selected the icons, click **Finish** to close the wizard and save the code as a MyBlock.

Define parameter inputs/outputs within the code

We are not finished yet! You will return to a screen showing your code, but now a grey block with four outputs will appear before the code. This is the final step of the parameter setup; you will use these data wires to tell the EV3 software where each of the inputs go in your code:

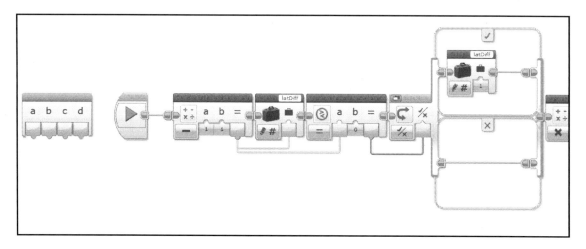

Recall that earlier we left the input of the subtraction blocks empty. Now, we will fill the empty inputs with the parameter data wires! The first math block calculates the difference in latitude. The subtraction order is destination position minus current position, so insert parameter **a** (curLat) as the second input of the math block, and insert parameter **c** (destLat) as the first input of the math block:

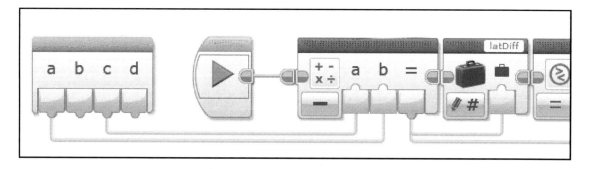

We will follow the same steps for the math block that calculates the longitude difference. Again, the subtraction order is destination position minus current position, so insert parameter **b** (curLong) as the second input of the math block and parameter **d** (destLong) as the math block's first input. When correctly configured, the input parameters should be wired like so:

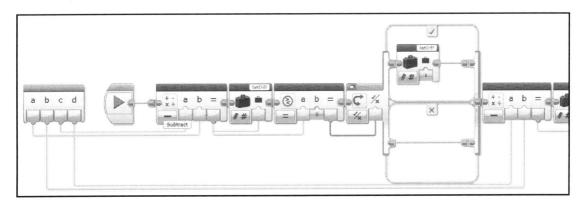

Earlier in this section, we discussed that you may need to add an extra math block that multiplies the position by –1. Remember that this extra step is only necessary for the latitude if you are located in the southern hemisphere and/or the longitude if you are in the western hemisphere. If you need this extra block, plug the parameter that holds the GPS reading into the multiplication block first. In this example, we added the multiplier to the longitude values, so parameter **b** gets multiplied by –1 before it is fed into the subtraction block. When this is put into place, the code will look like this:

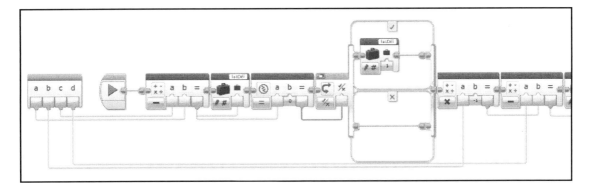

If you scroll to the end of your code, you will find another grey block, this time with an input. This is where you will inset the final output value so that it can be captured as the angle output parameter. Simply plug the data wire from the round block into the input of this grey block:

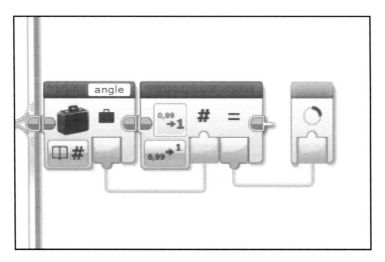

Parameter setup is now complete and the getAngle MyBlock is finished! When you add the MyBlock to a program, you will see the four inputs and a single output. When you hover your cursor over a parameter, its name will be displayed; keep this in mind, as it will help you avoid confusion:

Writing the program

Now that all five of the MyBlocks are finished, it is time to put them together to make the navigation program:

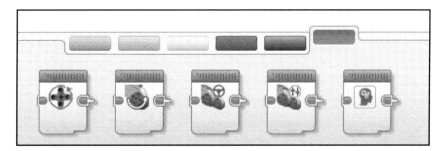

The first thing we need to do is define some variables. Create a new logic variable (set the mode to **Write | Logic**) and name it `exit`. Set its starting value to *false*. This variable's value changes to *true* when the GPS Car reaches its destination; this stops the navigation loop and ends the program:

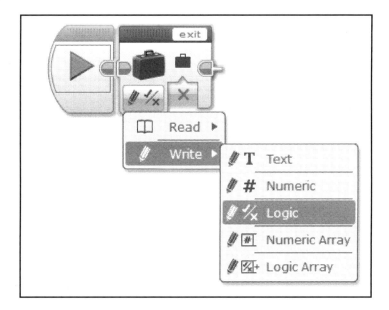

We need two more numeric variables named `destLat` and `destLong`. You will use these variables to set the destination coordinates. After these three variables, insert the `steerCenter` MyBlock so the GPS Car calibrates its steering mechanism before navigating. Lastly, add a loop. Later, we will change the loop's exit case so that the program exits when the `exit` variable's value changes to *true*:

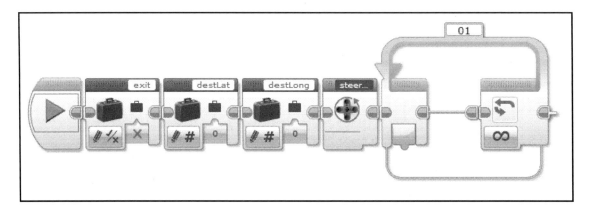

Refer back to the example coordinates for the Washington Monument that we acquired earlier. Its latitude is 38.889479 degrees, and its longitude is -77.035250 degrees. The latitude value will be entered into `destLat` as 38889479 and the longitude value will be entered into `destLong` as -77035250. When the values are entered into the variables, the EV3 software puts them into scientific notation and rounds the last digit. So, the coordinates become 3.888948e+07 for `destLat` and -7.703525e+07 for `destLong`:

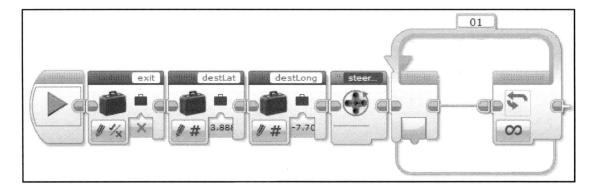

The first piece of code that we will place inside the loop is a move steering block (**On**, steering = 0, power = 75 percent). This turns on the drive motors so the GPS Car continuously powers forward while it navigates:

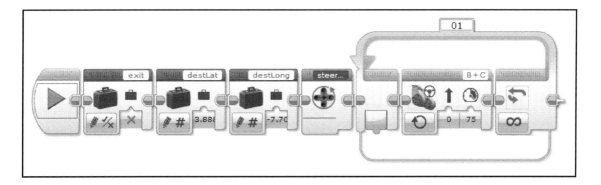

Next, we need to read our GPS position data. Insert two dGPS sensor blocks; set one to measure latitude and the second to measure longitude. Then, add two variable blocks with their modes set to **Read** | **Numeric** to retrieve the values stored in destLat and detLong:

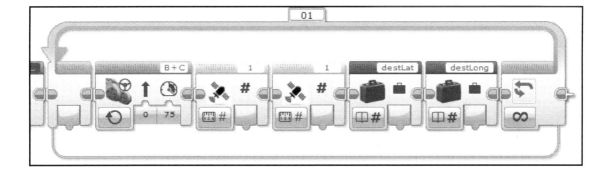

Add the `getAngle` MyBlock to the program and assign the sensor block outputs and variable values to the corresponding input on `getAngle`. The dGPS sensor block that reads latitude should plug into input **A** on `getAngle`; the dGPS block that reads longitude should plug into input **B**. The value of `destLat` should be assigned to input **C** and `destLong` should be assigned to input D. Using these input data, `getAngle` calculates an angle heading value, which indicates the direction that the GPS Car must turn to drive towards its destination; the `getAngle` output parameter, *angle*, stores the result of the MyBlock's calculations:

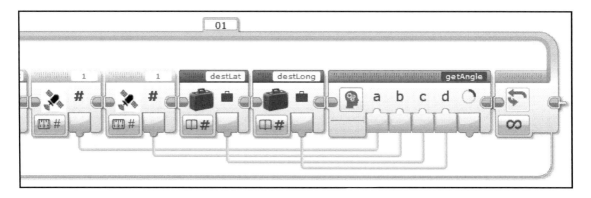

Now, it is time to put that heading value to use! Add a HiTechnic compass sensor block and change its mode to **Measure | Absolute Heading**. The programming block will reconfigure to include an input parameter; this input is used to set the target heading:

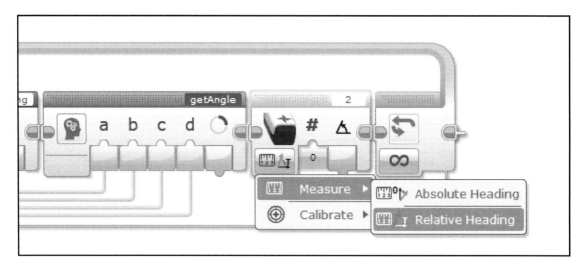

Plug the output of `getAngle` into the *target* input on the compass block. This sets the heading angle calculated using the GPS data as the compass's target heading. The compass will return a relative heading angle based on the target heading. Create a new numeric variable named `compassRelHead` and use it to store the compass's relative heading:

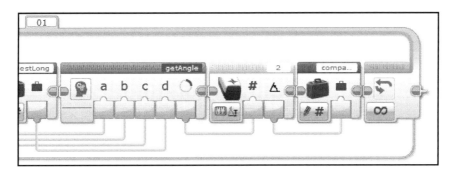

Earlier in the chapter, we established that the sign of the relative heading returned by the compass indicates the direction that the car must turn to reach its destination. If the relative heading is positive (greater than zero), the GPS Car must turn right; if the heading is negative (less than zero), the GPS Car must turn left. If the relative heading equals zero, no adjustment is required.

The program will first check to see if the relative heading is positive. This will require the usual programming with a compare block, which checks to see if the value is greater than zero, and a logic switch:

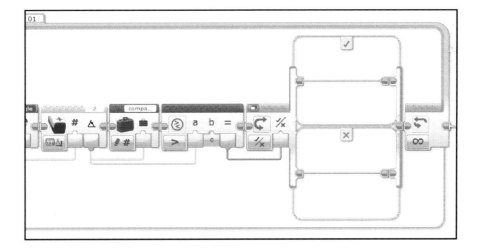

If the compare block returns *true*, the GPS Car must turn right to remain on course to the destination. Add the `steerRight` MyBlock to the *true* case of the switch:

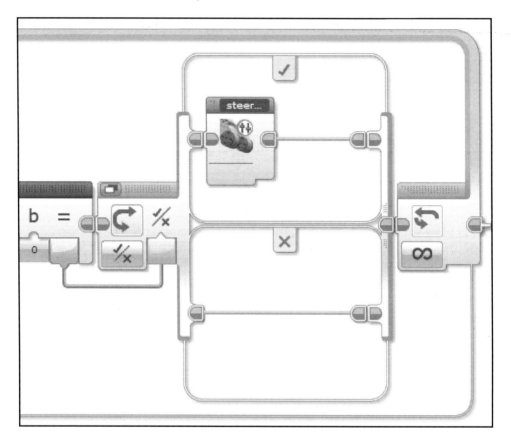

If the compare block returns a *false* value, then the program will check to see if the relative heading is negative. In the *false* case of the switch, set up a variable that reads the value of `compassRelHead`, checks to see if it is less than zero using a compare block, and returns its value to control a nested logic switch:

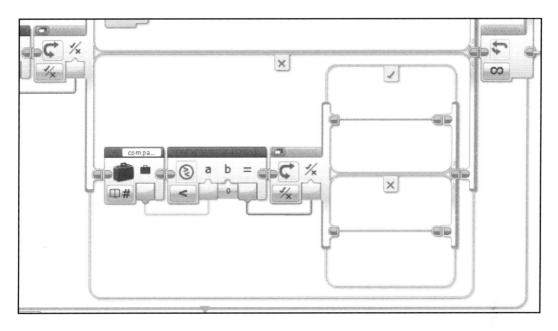

Place the `steerLeft` MyBlock in the *true* case of the most recent switch. The *false* case executes if the relative heading is equal to zero; place the `steerReCenter` MyBlock here:

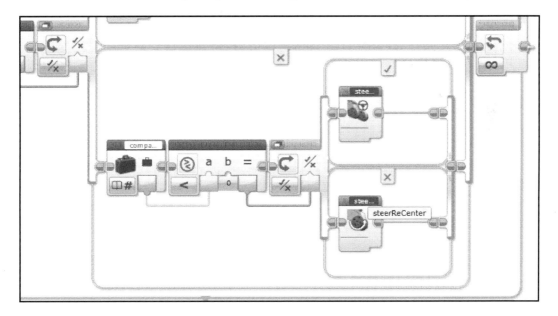

To prevent the EV3 from oversampling the dGPS, insert a wait block that will pause the program for a duration of one second after the switches:

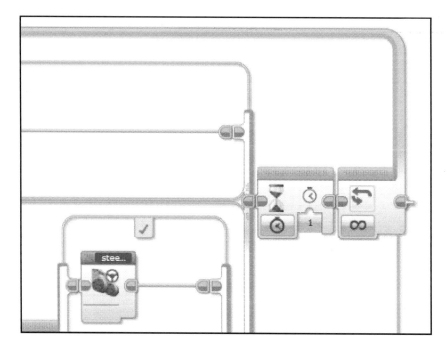

Only one more section of the program remains! The last piece of code compares the destination programmed by the user to the current GPS position and stops the program when it determines that the destination has been reached. It reads the values stored in latDiff and longDiff (recall that these values are calculated as an intermediate step within the getAngle MyBlock) and checks to see if they are within a certain range. This works because latDiff and longDiff are the distances to the destination in one dimension each. If both latDiff and longDiff are small, this indicates that the car is close enough, so the car stops and the program ends.

All variables defined in the EV3 software have a global scope. This means that they can be written to or read from any place in the program or even in a different program as long as they are from the same EV3 project file. The downside is that you must take careful consideration when naming variables; give every variable in the EV3 project file a unique name so that they do not interfere with each other.

The code will check the value of `latDiff` first. It reads the stored value and inserts it as the test value of a range block. The range block compares the test value to a predefined condition and returns a *true* or *false* value to indicate whether the test value meets the condition. Set the mode of the range block to **Inside** and set the lower and upper bounds to -10 and 10, respectively. In practice, this means that a *true* value will be the result if the car's current latitude is within roughly one meter in either direction of the destination latitude. The logic result of the range block will control a logic switch. You may set the switch to tabbed view because we will only write code in its *true* case. The code for the first half of the destination check looks like this:

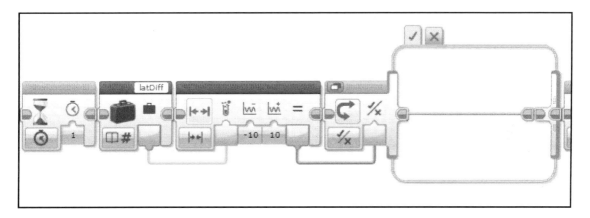

It is important that the code checks that the car is within range of the destination as opposed to checking to see if the current and destination coordinates match exactly. This is because the EV3 software rounds up the last digit of destination coordinates. Additionally, due of the inherent errors associated with GPS navigation, it is not reasonable to expect the car to reach the exact destination coordinates, which specify a location to a tenth of a meter. You can try adjusting the bounds of the range block; making the bounds wider will make the destination check less precise, but the car will find the destination more easily.

The second half of the destination check reads the value stored in longDiff, but otherwise, the code is the same. The second half of the check returns a *true* value if the car's current longitude is within one meter in either direction of the destination. The two halves of the destination check are nested as so:

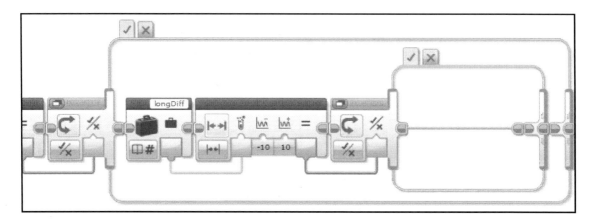

If both of these checks return *true*, then the car is close enough to the destination and the EV3 can exit the navigation loop. Add a variable block (mode set to **Write** | **Logic**) that changes the value of the exit variable to *true:*

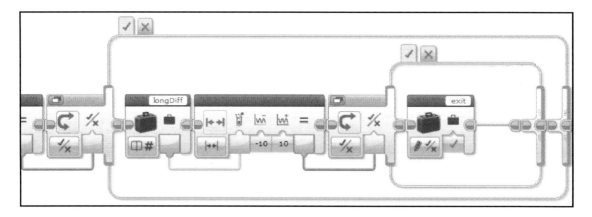

Change the exit case on the main loop to **Logic**. A loop in this mode will stop repeating when it receives a *true* value. Directly before the loop's exit case, add a variable block (mode set to **Read | Logic**) that reads the value stored in the exit variable. Plug the data wire from the variable block into the input of the loop block. This exit case occurs so that the navigation program repeats until the destination check changes the value of exit to *true*, causing the program to end:

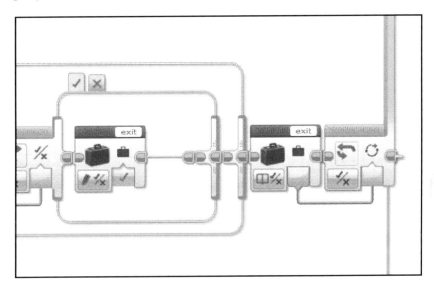

Finally, place two blocks outside the main loop: a move steering block (**Off**) and steerReCenter. When the car reaches its destination, it will stop and return its steering mechanism to the center position:

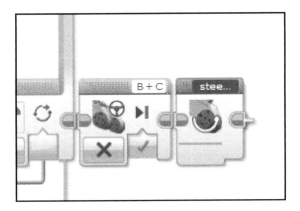

Putting it all together

When finished, the navigation program looks like this:

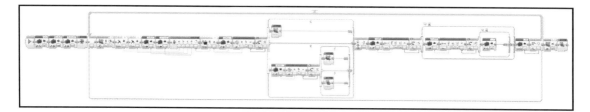

If you have made it this far and completed the program, celebrate a job well done! This was a difficult program to make, but you can hold your head high with the knowledge that you have completed a very smart piece of code!

Brainstorm some ways in which you can expand on the GPS car to make it smarter. For example, you can incorporate proximity sensors that allow the GPS Car to avoid collisions with obstacles.

Summary

We covered many new topics as we made our smartest robot yet.

We introduced two navigation sensors used by self-driving cars in the real world: the GPS receiver and the magnetic compass. We discussed how they work and learned about the basic principles behind using these sensors.

Before we started programming, we learned how to import third-party software into the EV3 software to allow us to use these sensors with the EV3. We wrote a simple program to test the GPS and get a feel for using the sensor. Then, we wrote a more sophisticated navigation program in which the EV3 used its GPS and compass to navigate to a pair of coordinates defined by the user. While programming, we expanded our knowledge of MyBlocks by introducing parameters, which allow you to program input and output for the MyBlock.

Congratulations! You have completed the final smart robot project. You are now ready to start building your own EV3 smart robots, as the principles that you learned while you built these six projects are now part of your engineering knowledge. You also have an understanding of the principles at work in a few real-world smart robots. I hope that this book has motivated you to start experimenting with more smart technology and inspired you to make something great!

Until next time, cheers!

Other Books You May Enjoy

If you enjoyed this book, you may be interested in these other books by Packt:

ESP8266 Robotics Projects
Pradeeka Seneviratne

ISBN: 978-1-78847-461-0

- Build a basic robot with the original ESP8266, Arduino UNO, and a motor driver board.
- Make a Mini Round Robot with ESP8266 HUZZAH
- Modify your Mini Round Robot by integrating encoders with motors
- Use the Zumo chassis kit to build a line-following robot by connecting line sensors
- Control your Romi Robot with Wiimote
- Build a Mini Robot Rover chassis with a gripper and control it through Wi-Fi
- Make a robot that can take pictures

Mastering ROS for Robotics Programming - Second Edition
Lentin Joseph, Jonathan Cacace

ISBN: 978-1-78847-895-3

- Create a robot model with a seven-DOF robotic arm and a differential wheeled mobile robot
- Work with Gazebo and V-REP robotic simulator
- Implement autonomous navigation in differential drive robots using SLAM and AMCL packages
- Explore the ROS Pluginlib, ROS nodelets, and Gazebo plugins
- Interface I/O boards such as Arduino, robot sensors, and high-end actuators
- Simulate and motion plan an ABB and universal arm using ROS Industrial
- Explore the latest version of the ROS framework
- Work with the motion planning of a seven-DOF arm using MoveIt!

Leave a review - let other readers know what you think

Please share your thoughts on this book with others by leaving a review on the site that you bought it from. If you purchased the book from Amazon, please leave us an honest review on this book's Amazon page. This is vital so that other potential readers can see and use your unbiased opinion to make purchasing decisions, we can understand what our customers think about our products, and our authors can see your feedback on the title that they have worked with Packt to create. It will only take a few minutes of your time, but is valuable to other potential customers, our authors, and Packt. Thank you!

Index

Made in the USA
Columbia, SC
13 November 2018